BULLYING AND THE BRAIN

Using Cognitive and Emotional Intelligence to Help Kids Cope

Gary R. Plaford

Rowman & Littlefield Education
Lanham, Maryland • Toronto • Oxford
2006

Published in the United States of America
by Rowman & Littlefield Education
A Division of Rowman & Littlefield Publishers, Inc.
A wholly owned subsidiary of The Rowman & Littlefield Publishing Group, Inc.
4501 Forbes Boulevard, Suite 200, Lanham, Maryland 20706
www.rowmaneducation.com

PO Box 317
Oxford
OX2 9RU, UK

British Library Cataloguing in Publication Information Available

Library of Congress Cataloging-in-Publication Data

Plaford, Gary R., 1947–
   Bullying and the brain : using cognitive and emotional intelligence
to help kids cope / Gary R. Plaford.
      p. cm.
   Includes bibliographical references.
   ISBN-13: 978-1-57886-395-2 (hardcover : alk. paper)
   ISBN-13: 978-1-57886-396-9 (pbk. : alk. paper)
   ISBN-10: 1-57886-395-3 (hardcover : alk. paper)
   ISBN-10: 1-57886-396-1 (pbk. : alk. paper)
   1. Bullying in schools. 2. Bullying. 3. Bullying in schools—
Prevention. I. Title.

   LB3013.3.P583 2006
   371.5'8—dc22

                                                        2005031280

♾ ™ The paper used in this publication meets the minimum requirements of
American National Standard for Information Sciences—Permanence of Paper
for Printed Library Materials, ANSI/NISO Z39.48-1992.
Manufactured in the United States of America.

CONTENTS

PART III   INTERNAL INTERVENTIONS STRATEGIES

INTRODUCTION

Aoccdrnig to rscheearch at Cmabrigde Uinervtisy, it deosn't mttaer in waht oredr the ltteers in a wrod are, the olny iprmoatnt tihng is taht the frist and lsat ltteer be at the rghit pclae. The rset can be a toatl mses and you can sitll raed it wouthit porbelm. Tihs is bcuseae the huamn mnid deos not raed ervey lteter by istlef, but the wrod as a wlohe and the biran fguiers it out aynawy. WOW!!!

—Unknown

How prevalent is bullying around the world? How prevalent is bullying in schools across the United States? As interesting as those statistics might be, they pale in significance to the question of how prevalent bullying is in your school. Have your students or your children been victims of bullying? Have they been bystanders when others were bullied? Have they perhaps been bullies themselves? In fact, what is bullying? What behaviors does it really encompass?

We all tend to think, "Not in my school, not with my child." We all want to believe that our school is special, that our school is different. Sit down. Brace yourself. The odds are that your school, that your child, is as much a part of the statistics on bullying as anywhere else.

Hard to believe? Ask the experts. The experts on bullying know. Who are the experts? When it comes to bullying in your home school, the experts are your own children. Your children know if bullying goes on, and more accurately, how much it goes on. They are the experts because they are living it.

As adults we cannot assume we know. We cannot afford to be naïve about this issue. We cannot afford to allow other adults to continue to be naïve about bullying in our schools. We cannot be afraid of what we might find out if we ask. We need to ask the experts what is really going on, and we need to believe them.

Finding the answer to that question raises some other interesting questions. If bullying is going on, why are so many adults in the dark about it? Why is it that so many children will not tell adults about bullying? If bullying is going on at our school, is it so bad? Won't it make children tougher? Shouldn't we let children work it out for themselves? Or should we do something about it? What effect does bullying actually have on children?

What effect does stress have on children? How does stress impact the developing brain? Is posttraumatic stress disorder directly related to childhood stress? What is the fight-or-flight response?

How exactly does the brain process stress, novelty, and routine? Are these functions processed in different areas in the brain? Can routine be used to manage stress? Can an individual shift the locus of control in the brain intentionally?

What part do emotions play in our daily decision making? What is motivation? How closely is motivation linked to emotion? Can motivation exist without emotion?

What is meant by emotional intelligence? How does emotional intelligence or the lack of it impact behavior? How does our psychological immune system influence our decisions and help us cope with those decisions?

What is the difference between grief and trauma? Where are emotionally charged memories stored in the brain? What is it about the way language is processed that makes it valuable as a tool for working with trauma?

How significant are connections in our lives? How significant are connections for children? What impact is our highly mobile society having on connections? How can we increase the likelihood of positive connections in the lives of our children?

How do all of these questions relate to bullying and victimization? What strategies can be drawn from what we are learning about the brain and about emotional intelligence that are useful in addressing this issue?

In their book *Bullying: The Bullies, the Victims, the Bystanders*, Harris and Petrie (2003) mention three strategies that need to be considered whether the bullying occurs in an elementary school, a middle school, or a high school. Those strategies include creating a climate that is affirming and safe, communicating appropriate behavioral standards to the student, and in some manner helping the student learn positive interpersonal skills. The first two of these, creating a climate and communicating standards, are what I call "external" interventions. The third strategy they mention, teaching positive interpersonal skills, is an "internal" intervention that can be useful for the bully, the victim, and the bystander. Internal interventions, as will be discussed in this book, include building positive interpersonal skills, but more broadly they involve building emotional intelligence and utilizing what we have learned about the brain and brain functioning to help us do just that.

Internal interventions for the bully include strategies that decrease the likelihood that he or she will bully again and decrease the need for the payoff the bully gets from bullying. Internal interventions for the victim include strategies that decrease the victim's susceptibility to being bullied and that help the victim respond to bullying in a way that does not promote continued victimization. In other words, internal interventions give bullies and victims the tools they need to better deal with their own emotions and the world they live in.

External interventions mean setting up external factors to educate and to monitor bullying. This includes creating a healthy climate and both setting and communicating appropriate behavioral standards, but it also includes getting the message out that bullying is not acceptable and will not be tolerated. This requires setting expectations and consequences for inappropriate behavior, including expectations for parents and teachers as well as for students. Expectations for students include not only expectations for the bully but also expectations for the victim of bullying and for bystanders.

Internal interventions are the internal tools we give bullies and victims to help them function better and be more successful in life and in dealing with others. They are designed to impact the brain and how it perceives and relates. External interventions are the ways and means of monitoring the behavior of students to negate the acceptability of bullying and the opportunity for it to occur in our schools. In honesty, however, everything we do impacts the brain. Consequently, external interventions will also have an impact on the way the brain functions.

It is important to understand that the brain is always changing. Everything we do changes the brain. When we start to develop habits of behavior, we are setting up neural pathways. Habits are behaviors, but they are not just actions or responses. The way we learn to perceive things or to think about things can also be habits . . . behaviors. A child's thinking, "I can't do it," can become a perceptual habit that is very destructive for that child. The brain, however, is a wonderful learning organ. It is designed to learn. It is designed to set up neural pathways . . . and it will do so very quickly. It is not designed to unlearn. That is why it is so very, very hard to break a habit. If you don't use a neural pathway for long periods of time, it will become weaker and weaker from disuse, and the habit may lesson in strength, but it does not go away. The best way to change a habit is to develop new neural pathways and intentionally use those until they are stronger than the old pathways . . . until you have replaced the old habit with a more potent new one. The old neural pathway will not be gone, but you will tend to use the stronger pathway instead. This information is very applicable to bullying, and we will discuss these applications more thoroughly in the second and third sections of this book.

The brain is truly a very remarkable organ. Think back to the first paragraph of this book, the one with most of the letters in the words out of place. Yet you could still read the paragraph. We can utilize this marvelous organ; we can engage this wonderful tool in addressing and decreasing bullying.

Part I
EXTERNAL INTERVENTIONS

①

WHAT PARENTS AND THE COMMUNITY MUST KNOW

One Sunday afternoon on a bright fall day a father was in charge of his young son. The son was happily playing and the father was happily reading the Sunday paper and watching the football game on the television. Then the son got bored and asked the father what he could do. The father, wanting to finish his paper and the game, decided on a task to keep his son busy. He had just noticed an ad with a map of the world in the newspaper. "Here is a map puzzle," he said. "I'll cut it up and you tape it back together. Come back when you're done and show me." That should keep him busy for a while, thought Dad as he settled back in his chair. Very soon, however, the boy was back, finished with the map. "How did you do that so quickly?" asked the father, a little disappointed but also impressed. "I turned the map over," said the boy, showing his father, "and when I did, this child was on the back. When I put the child back together the world was okay too."

—Unknown

PARENTS

As already mentioned, external interventions include expectations for parents, for educators and staff, and for students, with specific messages directed at bullies, at victims, and at bystanders. Everyone needs to know the expectations, the rules, and the consequences. Everyone needs a program. Everyone needs to be on the same page.

Parents are an integral part of setting up external interventions. Schools must take the time and make the effort to get the message out to parents and to the community, as well as to enlist their support. What is the message? The message includes several key parts. Just like baking a cake, leaving out any of the key parts—the key ingredients—will alter what we are serving up.

WHAT IS BULLYING?

The first message that a school must get out is the definition of bullying. What is bullying? Is it merely physical? Is it only striking, pinching, pushing, shoving, or touching another in an unfriendly, unwelcome, domineering manner? Is it also the threat or intimidation of doing these things? Does bullying also involve relational aggression, verbal abuse, verbal put-downs, harassment, jokes, or pranks at another's expense, intentionally embarrassing another, social ridicule, rumor starting, or social exclusion? Does bullying include passing intimidating notes? Does it include intimidating phone calls? Does it include harassing e-mails or threatening, harassing, or embarrassing web pages? Is bullying any behavior that uses threat, fear, intimidation, harassment, coercion, humiliation, or isolation to influence another person in a negative manner?

The fact is, bullying is at least all of the above. Harris and Petrie (2003) do a good job of summarizing the criteria cited by Dan Olweus (1993) defining bullying:

- It is aggressive and intentionally harmful.
- It is carried out repeatedly.
- It occurs in a relationship where there is an imbalance of power.
- It usually occurs with no provocation from the victim." (Harris & Petrie, 2003, p. 2)

When educators speak with parents or the community, they must make sure everyone is talking the same language (i.e., talking about and understanding the same issue). One way of doing this at a PTO meeting is to bring up examples of behavior and ask parents if they constitute bullying. Continue to bring up example after example of different ways kids have bullied or been bullied. It is even more effective if all the examples are of things that have occurred in your school. If they are, make sure parents are made aware that all these events have happened here.

Some parents may disagree with calling some of these behaviors bullying. If that happens, make sure you get them to think it over from the reverse perspective. In other words, would they call it bullying if it was happening to their child?

The bottom line is that the school should try to gain parents' support and make them aware of what behaviors constitute bullying. Short of that, it is at least necessary that the school has defined how it sees bullying, and how it will be categorizing these behaviors, and that appropriate discipline will be dispensed for these behaviors if and when they occur.

BULLYING DOES OCCUR AT OUR SCHOOL

The message that bullying occurs at your school is not a message that schools often want to admit. It sounds like a failure. It sounds as if the school employees are not protecting the children that have been placed in their care. It sounds bad, but it does not need to be a negative message if it is thoroughly explained. What needs to be explained is that your school didn't cause the problem, but your school wants to be a part of the solution.

The problem of bullying is occurring in schools across the nation. The fact is, bullying is being promoted in our society. A perfect example of this is professional wrestling. Take a close look at this form of entertainment. Professional wrestlers intimidate and bully each other, the so-called managers, the announcers, the audience. This behavior is not merely broadcast on television nearly every evening, but it is glorified as well. These wrestlers have become heroes for many young, impressionable children. Professional wrestling models bullying behavior, and our youth are learning from it. It would be a miracle if bullying was not occurring among our youth.

Besides wrestling, take a look at some of the rap music and heavy metal music that is produced for the benefit of our youth. The messages in these music forms are often threatening, demeaning, intimidating, and even violent. The messages often promote disrespect, harassment, and even violence toward others. Again, our youth are getting the message.

The amount of violence in movies and on television, which desensitizes children to violence in general, is another issue entirely. Although relevant here, it is beyond the scope of this book. It is enough to state that it is also a factor.

The message educators must get out to parents and the community is that bullying does occur in schools, and there are some factors that influence children to act this way (e.g., wrestling, rap music, and heavy metal music). In fact, one way of getting the point across at a PTA/PTO meeting is to tape a small segment of wrestling, where the wrestlers are intimidating and bullying, and show it at the meeting. Also, play some rap music or heavy metal music that promotes bullying, harassing, and intimidating behavior. Parents may not be able to or want to control everything their children watch on television or listen to on their CDs, but parents can and should discuss with their children the messages they are hearing.

If there is reluctance or potential reluctance to accept that bullying is really a problem, it may be useful to conduct a survey or questionnaire. This could be a stand-alone survey asking just a few simple questions of children about bullying. It could also be an add-on to an already existing survey. Many schools do drug surveys or other types of surveys. Adding a few questions about bullying is usually not very difficult. The questions that need to be asked should be simple and brief. This is not rocket science. The questions could include such things as the following:

1. Have you been bullied (hit, kicked, shoved, tripped, or threatened) within the past 30 days?
   __ No __ Yes If yes, how many times? __ 1 __ 2–3 __ 4–5 __ 6 or more

2. Have you had friends who have been bullied within the past 30 days?
   __ No __ Yes If yes, how many times? __ 1 __ 2–3 __ 4–5 __ 6 or more

3. Have you been harassed (teased, put down, called names, or touched in an uncomfortable manner) within the past 30 days?
   __ No __ Yes If yes, how many times? __ 1 __ 2–3 __ 4–5 __ 6 or more

4. Have you had friends who have been harassed within the past 30 days?
   __ No __ Yes If yes, how many times? __ 1 __ 2–3 __ 4–5 __ 6 or more

5. Have you been the victim of relational aggression (been left out, been ignored, had rumors started about you, been isolated, or been lied about) within the past 30 days?
   __ No __ Yes If yes, how many times? __ 1 __ 2–3 __ 4–5 __ 6 or more

6. Have you had friends who have been the victim of relational aggression within the past 30 days?
   __ No __ Yes If yes, how many times? __ 1 __ 2–3 __ 4–5 __ 6 or more

7. Have you been ridiculed (made fun of, had pranks or jokes played on you, teased, or been laughed at) within the past 30 days?
   __ No __ Yes If yes, how many times? __ 1 __ 2–3 __ 4–5 __ 6 or more

8. Have you had friends who have been ridiculed within the past 30 days?
   __ No __ Yes If yes, how many times? __ 1 __ 2–3 __ 4–5 __ 6 or more

9. Have you been harassed through notes, over the phone, or via e-mail or a web page over the past 30 days?
   __ No __ Yes If yes, how many times? __ 1 __ 2–3 __ 4–5 __ 6 or more

10. Have you had friends who have been harassed through notes, over the phone, or via e-mail or a web page over the past 30 days?
    __ No __ Yes If yes, how many times? __ 1 __ 2–3 __ 4–5 __ 6 or more

11. Please check all the places where these behaviors have happened.
    __ Classroom
    __ Playground
    __ Lunchroom
    __ Restroom
    __ Locker room
    __ At the bus stop
    __ On the school bus
    __ Other

SCHOOLS DO NOT CONDONE BULLYING

Although bullying does occur in your school, this does not mean the school condones it or that school personnel do not put a stop to it when they see it. One of the issues here is "when they see it."

Children will often do things behind the teacher's back. In the typical classroom in public schools, there is one teacher and anywhere from 20- to 30-some students. Sometimes there is an aide or a student teacher, but still the ratio is stacked against the staff. As much as we like to think teachers have eyes in the backs of their heads, they really do not. A child who wants to do something without the teacher seeing it has ample opportunity to do so if he or she is patient. When you add in all those times when there are even more children together, less structure, and fewer adults around (e.g., on the playground, at recess, in the lunchroom, at the bus stop), there are a multitude of opportunities for bullying to occur that will not be observed.

This means that educators must rely on being informed when bullying occurs. This, however, often does not happen. When children are the victims of bullying, they will often not tell a teacher or playground supervisor. Why don't they tell? There are several factors. First and foremost, sometimes when they do tell they are not believed. Second, there is the code of not "snitching" on each other. They do not want to be labeled as a tattletale by their peers. This "no-tattling mentality" is often reinforced by adults—both parents and teachers. Third, children also tend to believe either that if they ignore the bullying it might stop or that if they tell an adult the bully will find out and the bullying will get worse. This is often reinforced by the bully, who will threaten the victim. The bully conveys the message that if the victim tells, he or she will really "get it." This is a very powerful threat, especially if the bully is not one person but a group of several children.

Sometimes children will tell a sibling that they are being bullied, and parents find out. Or sometimes a child will tell his or her parents directly. Often, however, when a parent does find out, the child will plead with the parent not to tell the school. Children are terrified of getting hurt or bullied even more if the bully finds out they told. They may not want to go to school or even feign illness to stay home. This also places parents in a very awkward situation. What should a parent do? Do they risk that their child is right and is in jeopardy if they tell the school? Can the school protect their child? What is the best decision to protect their child?

The simple truth here is that bullying does not stop on its own. If ignored, it will continue and usually get worse. When school personnel learn about bullying, however, they can usually stop it. School officials will generally or should generally do two things: confront the bully and call the bully's parents. The goal is to put a stop to the bullying. The school has a progressive discipline structure in place, and if the bully continues with the behavior, the disciplinary interventions become continually more severe. Ultimately, a school will suspend and even expel a student who continues to bully others. In cases where the bully has been violent or threatened violence, referrals will also be made to the police or to the probation department. The fact is that bullying is like many other behaviors. It is done for a reason. The bully is gaining something from the behavior. If the situation can be altered so that bullies are losing more from continuing the behavior than they are gaining from continuing the behavior, the behavior will stop.

As a parent it is important to understand, and to help a child who is the victim of bullying understand, that the school and the people who work there are your allies. They don't want the bullying to go on, and they will help put an end to it if they know. It is equally important for educators to keep in mind that most parents do not want their children to be bullied, nor do they want them to be bullies. Parents are a wonderful resource to stop bullying, but they must be informed of the issues. If a parent learns that a child is being bullied, it is important to communicate this to the teacher or school principal. It is equally important to tell your children that if they are being bullied, they need to tell their teacher at school. Additionally, it is important to tell your children that it is not okay to bully or to participate in bullying. If they do so, there will be consequences. Finally, if they see someone else getting bullied, it is important to tell the teacher. When bullies get away with bullying one child, they will typically bully someone else later on. To not tell allows other children to become victims down the road.

CHAPTER SUMMARY/STRATEGIES

1. Have a discussion with parents so that everyone is on the same page as far as understanding what bullying is. It is best to give examples so that there is no question as to how the school is defining bullying behaviors.
2. Give the message loud and clear that bullying does happen at your school, and lead a discussion about some of the dynamics and influences in our culture that promote bullying and intimidating behavior.
3. If there is any doubt that bullying occurs, conduct a simple student survey regarding bullying and perceived school safety.
4. Let it be known very clearly that bullying behaviors are not acceptable in your school and that there are consequences for students when they are caught bullying.
5. Ask for help from parents in talking with their children about bullying. Give parents the message they need to give to their children. That message must include the idea that bullying is not acceptable, that there are consequences for bullying, that they do not want their children participating in bullying behaviors, and that if their children are victims of bullying or a bystander when bullying occurs they should immediately tell a teacher or other adult at school.
6. Ask parents to contact the school if they become aware of bullying activity, whether it directly involves their child or not.

2

WHAT EDUCATORS MUST KNOW

Six blind men encountered an elephant for the first time. One grasped it by the trunk, one by the tusk, one by the ear, one by the leg, one by the tail, and one encountered the elephant's body. When asked what an elephant was they all had a different story. As educators we must see the elephant in the classroom for what it really is.

—Adapted

DON'T IGNORE BULLYING

The very first step in addressing bullying is to not ignore it. What does that mean? First of all, that means opening your eyes. Bullying does exist, and it happens more than educators typically think it happens. This is true for several reasons. As cited earlier, children tend to hide their questionable behavior from adults. They will more than likely attempt to act out bullying types of behaviors when the teacher is not around or not watching. That is not merely typical bullying behavior; that is typical childhood behavior. They don't want to get caught, and children are often good at not getting caught. So for every act of bullying the teacher sees, how many have actually occurred? That is the question that as educators we must ask.

Additionally, educators are often not aware of the extent of bullying because it occurs in places and from sources they may not expect. There are some stereotypes of what a bully looks like and acts like. These stereotypes often picture a bully as someone with low self-esteem, with something to prove because he or she doesn't measure up in other ways. In fact, some of the latest research on bullying clearly indicates that many bullies are very popular students. A study by Jaana Juvonen (2004) of UCLA found that "kids who harass other kids typically aren't outcasts with low self-esteem. In fact, they tend to be better adjusted socially than the average middle school student, challenging the common assumption that bullies need ego boosters" (p. 20). Consequently, sometimes as educators we aren't looking in the right direction, and even when we see acts of bullying we may not recognize it for what it really is. This is no small matter, and it must be addressed.

It is not a popular idea to think that the bully may not always be the kid in trouble, the kid who doesn't do his homework, the kid who hangs out in the wrong places after school, the kid who gets caught with cigarettes, the kid who is dirty and smells bad. Unfortunately, the bully may often be the kid who is popular with other students and with teachers, the kid who plays on sports teams, the kid who turns in her homework, the kid whose parents come to parent–teacher conferences. That's the bad news. The good news is, if some effort is put into it, the bullying behavior of these kids can be turned around.

BE PREPARED TO ADDRESS BULLYING

Another important issue is that sometimes educators see something happen, or possibly only a fraction of what happened, and they are not sure it was bullying. The thinking often goes like this:

"If it really had been bullying, someone would be coming to me to complain." Unfortunately, that is not always true. For many reasons, children will often not tell the teacher or other staff. Some of these reasons include fear of reprisal, the "no snitch" or "no tattling" code, and the feeling of being alone and that no one can help.

Educators need to be ready and willing to address behaviors they see that might be or could be bullying. They don't need to be 100% sure it was bullying to intervene. It is very permissible, and really a good strategy, to intervene even when the educator is not sure what was going on. The intervention does not need to be disciplinary at this point. One approach would be to state, "I am not sure what I just saw. I am not sure whether this was bullying or not. If it was *not* then you have my apology, but if it *was* it needs to stop now! From this point on I will be watching more closely. If anyone has anything to say, they may do so now or come talk to me later." This message accomplishes several things. First it states to everyone involved that the behavior was noted, that the behavior will be watched, and that bullying is not acceptable and needs to stop; it also gives permission for the victim to speak up. The victim may not be able to say anything at that moment, again for fear of reprisal, but it opens the door for him or her to talk with the educator later on. If what occurred was not bullying, the speech was still not wasted. It still gave the message, educating students once again that bullying is not acceptable.

INTERVENTION BASICS

When bullying behavior is clearly noted as bullying, the educator must intervene, and there are some very precise steps that must be taken. Again, at this point, depending on the nature and severity of the bullying, the intervention need not necessarily be a disciplinary action. If the bullying is physically threatening to the victim, is clearly emotionally traumatic, or is in any way approaching these areas, then the intervention may need to be disciplinary in nature and may require an office referral. This is sometimes a judgment call, and if there is any doubt it would be better to err on the side of making an office referral.

However, in some cases the bullying has not been observed before by the educator (first-time event), or it is in the category of teasing or making the victim uncomfortable, but it is not what you would call serious or extreme. In these instances, the behavior may not require discipline but definitely requires intervention. If intervention does not follow, then the message is clear to the bully, the victim, and any bystanders that bullying is being condoned. The bullying behavior will then not only continue but will also likely grow worse over time. This leaves the victim in the victim's role, potentially causing emotional stress that can have clear negative implications for his education, for his achievement, and for his feelings about wanting to be in school. It makes school an unsafe environment for the victim.

Lack of intervention also places the bully in jeopardy. If the bully gets the message that bullying is condoned, his behavior may escalate in quantity and severity. When intervention does occur at some later point, as it surely will, it may be too late to do anything other than some form of suspension or expulsion. The bully's education could be put at risk because she was not given a clear message early on. This also places the school at risk of both being and being thought of as an unsafe environment by bystanders and other students, and ultimately by parents and the community at large. It also places the school at risk for potential lawsuits, which can become very sticky and uncomfortable.

So if there are clear and precise steps to be taken, what are they? First of all the bullying behavior must be clearly noted and addressed as bullying. The staff person who sees it must make it clear to everyone involved that the behavior has been observed: It is known, it is not secret, and it is bullying behavior.

The next step is to clearly state that the behavior is not acceptable. The bully, the victim, and all bystanders must get the message that this is not condoned by the school.

The third step is to inform the bully or bullies that the behavior must stop immediately and must not happen again. There are to be no recurrences of this behavior, and since it has been noted it will be watched for. This puts the bully on alert that he will be watched more closely.

Finally, everyone involved must understand that if the behavior does not stop immediately, or if it is observed again later on, a referral to the office and appropriate disciplinary actions will occur. This will include a phone call to parents. And if, in fact, the behavior does occur again, then the educator must follow through with that office referral.

To recap, the educator's intervention steps include the following:

1. The behavior is *known/seen*. (It is no longer undetected.)
2. The behavior is *not* acceptable. (It is not condoned.)
3. The behavior must *immediately stop*. (A direct command is issued.)
4. There are *consequences* if it continues. (Fair warning has been given.)

This intervention should be noted and dated somewhere in case the next step, an office referral, is necessary. If the situation does eventually reach the point of suspension or expulsion, this information is invaluable in making that case. The good news is, if these interventions are put into place, fewer and fewer situations will require suspension or expulsion.

These intervention steps are important for the bully to hear, but they are equally important for the victim to hear. The victim needs to know that the behavior has been noted, that it is not acceptable, that it is expected to stop, and that there are consequences if it does not stop. Victims should also be told directly that if this happens again, they can and should come and tell a teacher or some other adult. This gives them the support to know they are not alone. It lets them know it is not okay for others to victimize them at school or anywhere else. It lets them know that being a victim is not their fault. This could be eye-opening news for some victims.

CHAPTER SUMMARY/STRATEGIES

1. Don't ignore bullying. It does happen in your school, and it needs to stop.
2. Intervention does not have to be disciplinary in nature to be effective.
3. The following are the four key intervention steps with a bully:
   a. Let the bully and all other students know that the behavior has been seen and noted. It is not a secret.
   b. Let the bully and all other students know that bullying is not acceptable here.
   c. Let the bully and all other students know that the bullying behavior must immediately stop.
   d. Let the bully and all other students know that there will be consequences if it continues or happens again. Those consequences include discipline at school as well as a parent contact.
4. Let the victims of bullying know that it is not their fault, bullying is not okay, they are not alone, and they must report bullying if and when it happens to them.

WHAT STUDENTS MUST KNOW

There is a great battle that rages within me. One side is the soaring eagle. All that the eagle stands for is good and true and beautiful, and it soars above the clouds. Even though it dips into the valleys it lays its eggs on the mountaintops. The other side of me is the howling wolf. That raging, snarling wolf represents the worst that lies within me. The wolf feeds upon my downfalls and justifies himself by his presence in the pack. Who wins this great battle? The one I choose to feed!

—Unknown

BE PROACTIVE

If a school is to have a positive impact on bullying, then the school faculty and staff must take a proactive stance toward bullying. The staff must certainly be reactive when they either observe or learn about instances of bullying, but being reactive and ready to respond is not enough. Steps must be taken proactively to educate all students about some basic issues related to the problem. This does not have to be an add-on subject, it does not need to be an additional curriculum subject, and it does not have to be something extra. In most elementary classrooms, for example, there is a discussion of class rules at the beginning of the year. This may vary a little with middle school and high school classrooms, but there are still opportunities for a discussion of rules sometime, somewhere. When rules are discussed, take the opportunity to discuss bullying. Have a rule specifically stating that bullying is not allowed. These discussions can go far by just asking the class some specific questions.

What Is Bullying?

A great opening question for the class is simply "What is bullying?" Get the students thinking and talking about what it means and all the ways it can occur. Get them to give examples. A teacher can keep the conversation going for a long time just by continuing to ask the right questions. "Does bullying include harassment? Does bullying include jokes or pranks at another's expense? Can bullying be done via e-mail, phone calls, a web page? Does bullying include social isolation? Does bullying include starting rumors or telling lies about someone?" These questions help the students identify as many different forms of bullying as possible. The list should of course include the physical ways bullying occurs such as hitting, striking, pinching, shoving, tripping, grabbing, holding, or touching someone in a painful, threatening, unfriendly, unwelcome, demeaning, or humiliating manner. It also includes the threat of such physical action. The list must also include harassment, verbal abuse, verbal put-downs, social ridicule, and jokes or pranks at another's expense.

Bullying can also involve socially isolating other people, intentionally omitting or not including them, leaving them off the team, choosing them last for everything, starting rumors, and so on. The discussion should also include how bullying can occur. It can certainly occur face-to-face, but it can also start behind someone's back. It can occur over the telephone, via e-mail, or even through an embarrassing or humiliating web page. The roots of bullying can begin in a group discussion about someone who is not even present at that moment. Basically it can include any manner in which one or several people use fear, intimidation, harassment, threat, coercion, humiliation, or isolation to negatively affect another person.

Having this discussion with a class makes the students aware of what bullying really is, and it gets everyone on the same page in understanding the problem.

Why Does Bullying Occur?

Another key question to ask the class is why they think bullying occurs. What are the social factors that influence bullying? This part of the discussion could go on forever if allowed, but it does not need to. It is not important or possible to determine every contributing factor, but some should be discussed so that students realize there are social factors that influence bullying. A few specific ideas are always good to mention, such as the impact of the media. What are students exposed to on television, at the movies, on the radio, or on CD or MP3 players that influence bullying behavior? Included here should be the idea that violence in movies and video games desensitizes people to the violence they see in real life. Another significant topic is specific programs such as professional wrestling, where the athletes bully and intimidate each other and the behavior is glorified. Another could be the influence of some professional athletes who include bullying and intimidation as part of their strategy. Yet another would be the influence of some of the rap and heavy metal music that promotes violence or at least disrespect toward others. The goal here is not to try to convince students not to watch certain things or listen to certain music, but to open their eyes to the influence it can and does have on them and their peers and the effect this has in promoting bullying.

Another social issue to mention is the fact that students are widely varied in age. In elementary schools, there may be an age difference of 6 or 7 years between a first grader and a fifth or sixth grader. Middle school may consist of grades 6 to 8, 7 to 8, or 7 to 9, but even if it is only made up of two grades, there is still a definite size difference. In high school, freshmen are typically 4 years younger than seniors—and often quite terrified of them. This system of having children together in one building when there is such an age and size difference does not cause bullying, but it lends itself to it. A sixth-grade student who has been bullied throughout his educational career, and who has the mind-set to "return the favor" to others, certainly has multiple opportunities with all the younger children around. This can and does lend itself to the opportunity for bullying, but it also provides a chance to teach children a responsible and compassionate approach to those younger, smaller, and weaker than themselves.

What Does It Feel Like to Be Bullied?

One of the reasons for laying the groundwork regarding why bullying occurs is to be able to discuss what it feels like to get bullied. Some children may be reluctant to admit they were ever bullied, especially some "macho" boys. If, however, they can understand that it happens to a lot of others, and if they can grasp why it happens and how the age and size differences in schools can impact this, then it is not such an affront to the macho image some of the male students try to display to admit that they too have been bullied. If the pain bullying causes is going to be addressed openly, then all students must be willing to openly discuss it. If certain groups are hanging back and are not willing to discuss the issue, that will shut down the discussion others are willing to engage in.

The importance of open discussion is twofold. First, it lets everyone see how prevalent bullying is. Second, it opens up everyone's eyes to the pain bullying causes. This kind of awareness can go a long way in helping students curb their own tendencies to bully, but it is also critical in helping bystanders realize the effect bullying has and why efforts to stop bullying are crucial.

SPECIFIC MESSAGES

In discussions about bullying with a classroom full of students, there will be representation from three possible groups: students who have bullied others, students who have been bullied, and students who have been bystanders when bullying occurred to someone else. There are even divisions among the bystanders, including those who urge the bully on, those who are appalled, those who try to stop it, those who are merely interested, and those who are simply glad it isn't them being bullied. Some students will fit into several or even all of these groups. Specific messages must be given to each of these groups, but all students should hear all the messages. Victims need to hear what messages are given to bullies, bystanders need to hear what victims are being told, and so on.

What the Bully Needs to Know

Bullies and potential bullies need to know that bullying behavior is wrong. They need that message loud and clear. They need to know it is harmful to the victim, harmful to the learning environment and the sense of having a safe school environment, and ultimately harmful to themselves.

Bullies also need to know that bullying behavior will not be tolerated. They need to know that the school faculty and staff will be watching for such behavior, and that all students are being encouraged to report bullying behavior. The bully needs to know without question that if he bullies another student, he will get caught.

The bully needs to know that when she is caught, there will be consequences. These consequences must include progressive disciplinary actions at school and immediate notification of the student's parents or guardians.

The bully needs to get these messages clearly and needs to know without a doubt that the rules will be upheld. If bullying behavior goes unresponded to, if discipline does not follow, if parents are not contacted immediately, then the bully is being given the green light to continue.

What the Victim Needs to Know

In addition to hearing the messages directed toward bullies, victims need to have some specific messages for their ears. The first message they need to hear is that it is not their fault they are being bullied. This is not the same thing as saying there is nothing the victim can do to stop it. There are strategies victims can use in response to being bullied that can deter it, and there are strategies victims can learn that will make them less susceptible to becoming a victim. They definitely should not interpret this message as meaning they are helpless, but they do need to understand that being the victim of bullying is not their fault.

Second, the victim needs to understand that he is not alone. Being a victim is an alienating and isolating experience. It is very easy to feel alone. Certainly when bystanders see the bullying and no one does anything, this promotes feelings of isolation and alienation in the victim. Likewise, and even worse, when a faculty or staff member sees bullying and does nothing, the victim feels alone even in the most crowded of classrooms. Another aspect of this sensation of being alone as a victim comes from the very nature of being a child. Children often think that if they know something, everyone else knows the same thing. This happens with young children, and it continues to happen with some children (e.g., children with autism). The point is, if a child is regularly bullied, he thinks everyone else knows he is being bullied. Teachers really may not know, and there really may be very few bystanders who have seen it, but the victim may well believe that everyone else knows because it happens on a regular basis. This will tend to make the victim feel that no one cares, supporting his feelings of alienation, isolation, and being on his own in a cold and uncaring school.

A third message the victim must receive is that ignoring the behavior will not make it stop. The victim must be taught that if no intervention is forthcoming, the bully will generally continue the bullying behavior, and it will likely grow in frequency and severity. The victim needs to be taught that if she is a willing victim in one instance, others who observe this may also try to victimize her. The victim must be taught that a continual acceptance of being bullied has an impact on her own frame of mind as to being a continual victim. This point will be discussed more thoroughly in the next section of the book on internal interventions, but the message also needs to be included here. The real point of instructing the victim that bullying will not stop if ignored is to get her to take the next part of this step, which is to tell someone. Quite often the victim not only feels alone but also is afraid that if she tells on the bully, the bully will retaliate and make the victim's life even worse. The victim needs to understand that the only way to stop the bullying is to tell someone and keep telling people until someone listens. Helping the victim understand that she is not alone is a big step in giving her the courage to tell someone else what is happening.

A good scenario is to teach victims to utilize a strategy that has been used with young children to protect them from sexual abuse. We have spent much time and energy teaching children to "say no, get away, and tell someone." That strategy, that technique, that routine has helped children to be safe when they might otherwise have fallen victims in another way. Victims of bullying can likewise be taught to help themselves by stating to the bully, "No," or "Stop that," by then getting away from or out of the situation as quickly as possible, and by immediately telling the teacher or another adult what has just happened.

What Bystanders Need to Know

Even if a child never acts as a bully toward someone else, and even if he is fortunate enough to never become a victim, he will undoubtedly at some point be a bystander. Being a bystander ranges from merely walking by a scene where bullying is happening to standing there rooting for the bully to do more, from merely

knowing that a peer is being bullied to showing up behind the
school at 3 o'clock to watch the predicted event.

Bystanders sometimes think that the bullying event has nothing
to do with them. They sometimes think there is nothing they can
do. They are sometimes happy it is someone else getting bullied
rather than them. They sometimes watch to see what happens, if
anything, to the bully afterward. Ultimately, if repeated acts of bullying and violence are witnessed at school, bystanders will perceive
school as an unsafe environment. When enough students start to
think the school is unsafe, there becomes an atmosphere that is
less open, less friendly, and not as conducive to educational tasks
and educational achievement.

What bystanders need to know—and keep in mind that bullies
and victims are also bystanders at times—is that they do have
power, and there are things that can and should be done. Bullying
often occurs not just because the bully needs to bully but also because the bully wants a crowd to watch the event. This means that
each bystander has options . . . and some power. The options perceived may be influenced by a bystander's own fear of the bully,
but there are options. One option is to walk away, to refuse to
watch. In fact, one bystander can encourage other bystanders to
also walk away. If it is not a dangerous situation where the bystander perceives he could quickly become another victim, then
the bystander can also help to shift power. In other words, the bystander can point out that the bullying behavior is not called for
and that the bully should stop it immediately.

Another action a bystander can take is to support the victim. After a peer has been victimized by a bully, a bystander can talk to
the victim, let the victim know that what happened was not right
and that it was not her fault, let the victim know she is not alone,
encourage the victim to tell someone about the incident, go with
the victim to report it, and corroborate the victim's story.

A final strategy any bystander can and should take is to make
sure the incident is reported immediately. Whether he says anything to the victim or not, the bystander should report the bullying

incident to a teacher or other staff. And if nothing is done or it appears nothing will be done, he should keep on reporting it until someone listens and acts.

Bystanders are not powerless in these situations. By not taking a passive role, by not condoning bullying, by supporting the victim instead of the bully, and by reporting bullying acts every time they are witnessed, a bystander can have a significant influence on the environment at a school. A bystander can help make school a safer place for all students. This could be a wonderful project for the student council.

CHAPTER SUMMARY/STRATEGIES

1. Have classroom discussions about what bullying is. Ask students to give examples.
2. Discuss why bullying occurs.
3. Discuss how it feels to be bullied.
4. Discuss the need to stop bullying at your school.
5. Give bullies or potential bullies the following message:
   a. Bullying is wrong.
   b. Bullying will not be tolerated at this school.
   c. There will be consequences for bullying behaviors.
6. Give victims the following message:
   a. It is not your fault.
   b. You are not alone.
   c. Ignoring the behavior will not make it stop.
   d. You need to tell someone.
   e. A good strategy is to "say no, get away, and tell someone."
7. Give bystanders the following message:
   a. Bullying affects everyone.
   b. Bystanders have power.
   c. Walk away; don't condone bullying by watching.
   d. Support the victim.
   e. Tell a faculty or staff member immediately.

Part II
INTERNAL INTERVENTIONS
ISSUES

4

BULLIES AND VICTIMS

Teachable moments are all around us if we just open our eyes. Imagine something like this. Your 4-year-old child wants to demonstrate a little independence, so he opens the refrigerator door and takes out the gallon jug of orange juice to pour his own glass. The jug is too heavy for him, he drops it, and orange juice starts spilling all over the kitchen floor. The child doesn't know what to do so he just stands there frozen to the spot. At that moment you walk in. You have a choice to make. Which is more important, the orange juice or your child? Far too often we go for the orange juice. This is a teachable moment, and you can be sure your child is learning from it. Life is a teachable moment.

—Adapted From Stephen Glenn

EDUCATING BULLIES AND VICTIMS

Besides external interventions—the external steps taken to monitor and control bullying—steps must be taken to give both the bully or potential bully and the victim or potential victim the skills and tools necessary to decrease bullying. What is meant by *potential bully* and *potential victim*? That refers to all the other students around. The bystanders, whether they are sidekicks, defenders, or onlookers, are all part of this group.

Internal interventions may be mainly directed at the bully or the victim, but many of the interventions can and should be done in classrooms. This will benefit all students. Why is this important? It is important because bullying thrives in a culture of secrecy. Getting it out into the open is the first step in controlling it. It is important because bullying occurs in a social context, and therefore it affects the entire school milieu. It is important because peers come into their own in adolescence, and it becomes of paramount importance to fit in at this age. The power of acceptance and rejection during adolescence is a driving force. Therefore, bystanders can play a critical role in solving the problem of bullying if we utilize peer pressure in the right way. If we allow the bully to be the compelling force in peer pressure, then the climate of bullying will continue. If we develop a climate where bystanders are the driving force in peer pressure, and can educate other bystanders to support a climate of caring, acceptance, tolerance, and peaceful coexistence, then a more positive, nonbullying climate will eventually prevail.

Sometimes there is much thought given to dealing with the bully, but no thought that the victim also needs to be addressed. Being victimized by bullying on a continual basis does not make one stronger or help a "boy become a man" as some of the street philosophy espouses. On the other hand, it may actually decrease the ability to deal with stress later on in life. This will be discussed in a later chapter. The point is we need to deal with both the bully and the victim (and all the potentials). This means giving the bully skills and tools that will decrease his or her desire, need, and inclination to behave in a bullying manner. It means giving the victim skills and tools that will decrease his or her susceptibility to bullying and his or her behaviors that tend to elicit bullying from others. For both the bully and the victim, this involves raising their level of emotional intelligence, it involves building and strengthening connections, it involves finding and creating new options and alternatives, and it involves building new strategies based on what is now known about emotional intelligence and brain research.

WHY EMOTIONAL INTELLIGENCE?

Daniel Goleman (1995) discusses the five domains of emotional intelligence in his book *Emotional Intelligence: Why It Can Matter More Than IQ*. The domains include understanding one's own emotions or self-awareness, managing or having some control over one's own emotions, being able to motivate oneself and delay gratification, recognizing emotions in others and being able to feel empathy for others, and building and maintaining social relationships. Emotional intelligence needs to be addressed in the bully because the bully often demonstrates a deficit or lagging development in emotional intelligence. The bully often has no understanding of how her behavior impacts others. She has no concept of how others are feeling. There is no empathy for the plight of others. The ability to empathize is a sign of a higher level of or growing level of emotional intelligence, and bullying is often a sign that there is no empathy. And finally, there is little or no understanding of how to build or maintain appropriate social relationships.

Emotional intelligence needs to be addressed in the victim because the victim also often demonstrates a deficiency in that realm. It is true that a person may become a victim for a variety of reasons. Sometimes it is because he is in a minority situation racially, ethnically, or religiously. It may also occur because the victim has some individual trait such as a limp or a hearing aid that causes him to stand out. It is also very true, however, that a person is often a victim because he has demonstrated a lower level of emotional intelligence. The victim often has little understanding of his own emotions, how to control or manage his own emotions, or how others interpret his emotions and his behaviors. He also often lacks an understanding of how to build or maintain social relationships. You can hear indications of this if you listen closely to what students say. "Watch me make him cry," "watch me make him angry," "watch me get him into trouble," "watch me pull his string," or "watch me push his buttons" are indications that others have noticed a lower level of emotional intelligence in the proposed victim. This victim will be victimized wherever he goes because the lagging emotional intelligence is easy to recognize. Increasing the level of emotional intelligence will not only decrease the victim's susceptibility to being bullied up front but also alter the manner in which the victim responds to bullying if and when it does occur and decrease both the severity of the event and the likelihood it will happen again.

In this day and age when schools must think about safety issues, bullying, school violence, and so on, it also must be kept in mind that it is the victim who will bring a gun to school. The bully has no reason to do so. It is the victim who feels the need to get even. If we have learned one lesson from the school shootings that have occurred, and the ones that have been narrowly avoided, it is that it is the students that have been bullied, harassed, alienated, isolated, humiliated, and terrorized who will bring a gun to school to get even with those that have subjected them to these indignities.

Building emotional intelligence, creating positive connections, and finding different alternatives and strategies for our students may sound like a daunting task, but it is not as difficult as it at first might seem. Some of the latest brain research is pointing the way. All we need to do is open our eyes, sharpen our senses, and follow the yellow brick road.

CHAPTER SUMMARY/ISSUES

1. Besides monitoring bullying externally, we need to teach internal strategies and skills to be effective in this endeavor to reduce or stop bullying in our schools.

2. These internal interventions must address both the bully and the victim.

3. These internal interventions must address potential bullies and potential victims, which means all bystanders.

4. Bullying happens in a social context, and peers come into their own in adolescence.

5. Children's dependence on peers can be used as a strategy in dealing with the bullying issue.

6. Emotional intelligence is a critical component in helping the bully not to be a bully.

7. Emotional intelligence is a critical component in helping the victim not to continue to be a victim.

8. In providing a safe school environment for all students, it is not just the bully and victim who are at stake. Keep in mind that it has always been and always will be the victim, not the bully, who brings a gun to school to get even.

BRAIN RESEARCH

We learn:
10% of what we read
20% of what we hear
30% of what we see
50% of what we both see and hear
70% of what we discuss with others
80% of what we experience personally
95% of what we teach to someone else.

—William Glasser

THE BRAIN—WHAT IS IT?

The brain, of course, is that gray lump of fatty tissues housed inside our skulls. It stores memories. It does our thinking. It controls nonthinking body functions as well, like our breathing and heart rate. But it does a lot more than that. Certain parts of the brain perform certain functions. Dr. Daniel Amen, author of *Change Your Brain, Change Your Life* (1999), does a wonderful job of describing the functions and the problems of the different parts of the brain.

To be succinct, the limbic system is the emotional center of the brain. More specifically, it performs such tasks as storing highly charged emotional memories, it determines one's emotional tone and colors events emotionally, it promotes bonding, it controls motivation, it processes the sense of smell, and it monitors appetite and sleep cycles.

When there are problems in the limbic system, we might observe negative thinking, negative perceptions, and negative emotions. Moodiness, irritability, lack of motivation, and increased social isolation are also evident. There will also often be problems with appetite and sleep patterns.

The basal ganglia are structures that surround the deep limbic system. They are involved with integrating feelings and movement, such as when we become paralyzed with fear. They are also important in determining the body's anxiety level, monitoring pleasure, and enhancing motivation. The basal ganglia also control fine motor behavior.

When there are problems with the basal ganglia, we might perceive anxiety, nervousness, or panic. We might see physical sensations of anxiety, muscle tension, tremors, fine motor problems, or tics. We might also notice a tendency to think the worst, avoid conflict, and not have much motivation.

The prefrontal cortex is basically the front third of the brain. It controls attention span, perseverance, impulse control, judgment, self-monitoring, problem solving, critical thinking, organization, and learning from experience. It also interacts with the limbic system and monitors the ability to express emotions and empathy. The prefrontal cortex typically is considered to monitor the executive functions of the brain.

When there are problems with the prefrontal cortex, we will see impulse control problems, lack of perseverance, short attention span, distractibility, disorganization, procrastination, poor judgment, short-term memory problems, and trouble learning from experience. We might also observe many misperceptions and social anxiety.

The cingulate gyrus is a part of the brain that passes front to back through the deep part of the frontal lobes. This area allows us to shift our attention, to be flexible cognitively, to be adaptable, to see different options, and to cooperate.

When there are problems with the cingulate gyrus, we will see problems with getting stuck on ideas (obsessions), getting stuck on behaviors (compulsions), holding onto past wrongs, worrying, argumentativeness, uncooperativeness, addictive behaviors, eating disorders, and oppositional behavior.

The temporal lobes are the areas on the sides of the brain at the temples. The temporal lobes are split in function. Typically the left side is critical in understanding language, word retrieval, auditory learning, visual and auditory processing, immediate and long-term memory, and emotional stability. The right temporal lobe is typically critical in rhythm, music, visual learning, decoding intonation, and recognizing facial expressions.

When there are problems with the left temporal lobe, we might observe language problems, word-finding problems, reading difficulties, auditory processing problems, dark and violent thoughts, aggression, sensitivity to being slighted, and emotional instability. Problems with the right temporal lobe typically include difficulty with social skills, difficulty recognizing facial expressions, and difficulty decoding vocal intonations.

With all these areas of the brain, a key advancement in treating problems is the ability diagnosticians now have to look at what the brain is doing. Dr. Amen, as part of his psychiatric practice, looks at many of the disorders of the brain by using SPECT imaging. This allows us to see the blood flow in the brain, and basically what areas are getting too little or too much blood flow, which then gives indications for what medications might best increase or decrease activity in those areas. And beyond medications, it can give us clues as to how to intervene with behavioral and cognitive therapies. This is quite a step forward in technology, as well as a huge benefit in helping us deal with the brain when it is not functioning to the individual's best advantage.

NEW IDEAS

It seems that every year more and more is being learned about our brains. In *The Executive Brain*, Dr. Elkonon Goldberg (2001) discusses some recent discoveries about how the brain functions. He states that for a long time it was believed that the locus of control of certain functions of the brain were located in different hemispheres. For example, the locus of control of language was thought to be in the left hemisphere. The locus of control of functions such as mathematics or music were thought to be in the right hemisphere. This seemed to be confirmed by observable information. When an adult had a stroke in the left hemisphere of the brain, it was devastating to the individual's language. A stroke of the same magnitude in the right hemisphere, while impacting other functions, did not impact language in the same way as a left hemisphere stroke.

Then practitioners started to note the impact of a stroke in children. Since there are typically fewer strokes in children than there are in adults, and since no one was especially watching for differences, it wasn't immediately apparent. What was eventually noticed, however, was that in a child it was a stroke in the right hemisphere that was devastating to language.

That raised some interesting questions. If the locus of control of language is in the left hemisphere, how is it that a stroke in the right hemisphere instead of the left hemisphere of a child's brain impacts the child's language? This started some interesting research. One aspect of this research involved neuroimaging, where they can actually look at what part of the brain is triggered into action or lights up when certain functions are called upon.

The resulting knowledge from this research has incredible implications. What is now understood is that the locus of control of certain functions of the brain will shift from one hemisphere to another. This leads to an entirely new level of understanding of how the brain is set up to function. Novel functions, new ideas, and creative thought tend to be processed in the right hemisphere. Routine functions, patterned approaches, and habitual operations tend to shift to and are controlled from the left hemisphere.

The locus of control of language is now understandable. In adults, language is a routine function. Adults know the language they speak. An adult may learn a new word now and then or pick up a new way of using a word, but basically an adult's language is a routine function. Therefore, the locus of control of language in an adult is in the left hemisphere. For a child, on the other hand, language is novel. Almost every day a child learns new words, or new meanings for words, or that a word may mean different things in different circumstances. The child is regularly learning idioms and puns, jokes, and plays on words. Consequently, language is processed in the child's right hemisphere. At some point, when enough language is mastered that it becomes routine, the brain will gradually shift the locus of control to the left hemisphere.

This brings up some interesting questions. One issue that has long been noted concerns stuttering. Some children experience a degree of developmental stuttering when they speak. Some of these children, however, will simply outgrow this stuttering. Why do they outgrow it? No one has been able to answer that satisfactorily to this point. Is it possible that the "outgrowing" of their problem really has more to do with the shift of locus of control of language? Specifically, is it possible that there is some issue causing the child to stutter when language is being processed in his or her right hemisphere, but when the shift to the left hemisphere occurs the child no longer stutters? In other words, is it the shift itself that cures the problem?

Then what about adults who stutter? Consider Mel Tillis, a wonderful country and western singer. He does not stutter when he sings. The lyrics to a song are routine; they are the same every time he sings them. When he speaks, however, he stutters noticeably. Is it possible that in adults who stutter, the shift of the locus of control of language has something to do with this, or is the problem something entirely different? The fact that the locus of control shifts when processes become routine raises some interesting questions and possibilities.

Another issue now noted is that musical abilities are not necessarily located in the right hemisphere as was previously thought. For most of us they are. For real musicians, however, it is now understood that the locus of control has shifted to the left hemisphere because processing music has become routine for them.

This revolutionary concept that the locus of control of functions actually shifts from right to left as our actions become routine is very interesting, but it goes far beyond merely being interesting. It has incredible implications in many arenas. Some extremely significant implications involve strategies that will be addressed in the next section of this book. We will be coming back to this right–left, novelty–routine hemisphere issue shortly.

CHAPTER SUMMARY/ISSUES

1. The brain is made up of many different areas, and these areas perform different tasks. We are learning what some of those specific tasks are.
2. The limbic system is the emotional center of the brain. It triggers fear and anxiety, and it stores highly charged emotional memories.
3. The basal ganglia integrate our feelings with movement. They determine the body's anxiety or stress level.
4. The cingulate gyrus allows us to shift our attention, to be flexible, and to be adaptable.
5. The prefrontal cortex controls the body's executive functions, including attention span, problem solving, and organization.
6. The left temporal lobe controls language and word retrieval in adults.
7. The right temporal lobe controls rhythm and music for most of us.

8. SPECT imaging allows us to look at blood flow in the brain to see how the brain is functioning and what areas are underactive and which are overactive.

9. The locus of control of certain functions of the brain will shift. We process new information in the right hemisphere, but the control of routine information shifts to the left hemisphere.

10. Language may be an example of this phenomenon. It appears that in children language is processed in the right hemisphere because of the novelty of learning language, but for adults the processing of language shifts to the left hemisphere as it becomes routine.

11. The fact that novel processes are controlled in the right hemisphere and routine processes shift to the left hemisphere is more than merely interesting. It has significant implications in many arenas.

6

EMOTIONAL INTELLIGENCE

Time is all too precious. We make time, save time, spend time, waste time, borrow time, budget time, invest time, manage time, until we eventually call time-out. We now claim there is quality time. But can love be measured by seconds or minutes? Can human relationships be made warm in the microwave of quick encounters? We cannot care for children in convenient time; we can't learn from our elders in convenient time; we can't maintain marriages in convenient time. The result of adjusting our lives to the fiction of time will inevitably be empty adults, lonely elders, and neglected children.

—Steve Charleston

EMOTIONAL INTELLIGENCE DEFINED

There is a great deal of correlation between issues of emotional intelligence and issues such as bullying. If bullying is to be addressed with any real intent of decreasing it, the bully and the victim must both be helped. What they need in the way of help is for adults to promote, teach, and develop aspects of emotional intelligence within them. In lay terms, emotional intelligence means having an understanding of your own emotions, it means understanding how your emotions affect you, it means being able to put labels on your emotions and being able to express your emotions and to explain and discuss what you are feeling to others, it means being able to understand how your thoughts and actions impact your emotions and how your thoughts and actions impact other people's emotions, it means being capable of and expressing empathy for others, and it means having a sense of control over your emotions. This does not mean you are in control 100% of the time; it merely means you are not typically out of control.

The ability to put labels on your emotions is a significant skill. Some children (and some adults) have a very limited emotional vocabulary. They may know basically little more than *mad*, *glad*, and *sad*, thereby limiting their ability to express what they are feeling. In reality, however, it does much more than limit their ability to express feelings. In fact, it limits their ability to understand their feelings. If a child does not understand the difference between being angry and being frustrated, that child cannot manage or cope with that emotion adequately. You cannot manage your anger unless you have a clear concept of what you are trying to manage. A limited emotional vocabulary also limits an individual's ability to feel empathy. If one cannot understand what another person is feeling, it is impossible to feel empathy for that person.

Another aspect of emotional intelligence is that it is learned, typically through observation. In other words, it is modeled. However, aspects of emotional intelligence can also be taught. Now that the significance of emotional intelligence is beginning to be understood, it is becoming imperative that steps are taken to teach it. It is very difficult for children to learn and develop emotional intelligence if they grow up in homes where emotional intelligence is not being modeled. Unfortunately, this is the case in a growing number of homes. In our fast-paced, high-tech, high-stress society, parents spend an ever-decreasing amount of time in meaningful interaction with their children. The latest surveys quantify that time in terms of only minutes a day. The time we spend with our children is critical. Spending real time with our children is far more important than soccer practice, swim practice, time at the mall, and movie time. That isn't to state all those experiences do not have merit, but if and when these activities leave only microwave instants to connect with our children, then we have lost sight of what is really of importance.

There is ample evidence that the number of children for whom emotional intelligence is not being modeled, or not being modeled sufficiently, is growing. It is therefore critical that we take determined steps to counter this trend. Those steps include both promoting opportunities for modeling emotional intelligence and teaching certain aspects of emotional intelligence.

EMOTIONAL INTELLIGENCE AND THE CONTINUUM

With the understanding that emotional intelligence is learned comes the notion that an individual's level of emotional intelligence is on a continuum, just like measurements of one's intelligence quotient, or IQ. The main difference is that one's IQ would remain relatively fixed over time, while one's emotional intelligence, since it is learned, should increase over time. In other words, a child's or teenager's emotional intelligence level should go up as he or she gains experience.

Another way of looking at this is to understand that as a group, children and teens are on the lower end of the emotional intelligence continuum. Observing the manner in which children and teens interact with each other makes this point. The behavior of middle school girls is a prime example. They can and often do treat each other horribly. In fact, there are national projects directed at this very issue. The Ophelia Project, which is designed to address relational aggression in teenage girls, is a clear indication that there is a problem among middle school girls. Another indication of lower emotional intelligence is notable in the lack of ego strength.

Those who have worked with middle school girls may ask the question, "How many middle school girls does it take to go to the rest room?" They don't do this individually but rather as a herd, unless it absolutely cannot be avoided. There is nothing wrong with that. It is normal development. But it is also a sign that ego strength is not developed, which is clearly an aspect of emotional intelligence.

If middle school boys are observed, similar behaviors can be noted. They often tease, taunt, and bully each other mercilessly. As teenagers move into high school, emotional intelligence continues to develop and there is a definite change in behavior. The teasing, taunting, and bullying behavior decreases. It has usually decreased more in seniors than it has in freshmen. As youth move into college age, there continues to be growth, which is reflected in a continued decrease in bullying behaviors.

If we agree that children and teens as a group are on the lower end of the continuum of emotional intelligence, it is equally worth noting that children and teens who bully as well as those who are bullied tend to be even lower on that continuum. The behavior of both bullies and victims demonstrates this.

If we are to effectively address the issue of bullying, therefore, it is necessary to address both bullies and victims by setting up means whereby emotional intelligence can be modeled and taught. This is crucial if schools are to be made safe. Finally, as mentioned previously, it is not the bully who will be the one to bring a gun to school . . . it will be the victim. In all the known instances of school shootings, it was a child or children who were victimized who came back with weapons to even the score.

CHAPTER SUMMARY/ISSUES

1. Emotional intelligence is a crucial issue in both the control and prevention of bullying.
2. Emotional intelligence refers to the ability to understand and express emotions, to be in control of emotions, and to under-

stand another's emotions and be capable of feeling empathy for another.

3. Emotional intelligence is learned typically through modeling, but it can also be taught.

4. In many homes today emotional intelligence is not being modeled. The time spent in meaningful interaction between parents and children has significantly decreased over the years.

5. Looking at emotional intelligence as a continuum, children and teenagers are at the lower end of that continuum.

6. If children and teens are at the lower end of the emotional intelligence continuum, children who bully and victims of bullying are at the lower edge of that group.

7. To address the bullying issue, schools and parents must set up multiple possibilities for modeling emotional intelligence, and schools and parents must set up a systematic way of teaching emotional intelligence.

8. To successfully address the bullying issue, schools and parents must address the victim in addition to addressing the bully.

7

EMOTIONAL INTELLIGENCE AND DECISION MAKING

You cannot change the past, but you can start from right now and create a whole new ending.

—Zig Ziglar

THE EMOTIONAL INTELLIGENCE CONNECTION

Understanding the real significance of emotions in our lives is critical for understanding the importance of building emotional intelligence in our children and students. Emotions are not just some side event in our lives. It is not as if we think and we act, and, oh, by the way, sometimes we have emotions that result from our thoughts and actions. It is not nearly that simple. In truth, our emotions play an integral part in how we act, what we think, and how we make decisions. In fact, emotions are the driving force behind our decisions.

THE DECISIONS WE MAKE

We make many, many decisions every day. We make little decisions, and we make big decisions. Often the little decisions that we
make consistently will become our big decisions. If every morning
we decide to wait until tomorrow to take a certain action, then in
truth we have made a decision to not take action.

One decision many of us make is that of a marriage partner.
How do we decide whom to marry? This is an emotional decision.
Some people may decide to marry for money or status. They may
claim they do not care what their chosen mate will look like, act
like, or smell like; how they got their money; or what they do for a
living. In reality, very few people really do that. For most of us this
decision is based on our emotions—very strong emotions. Have
you ever known a couple getting married that you knew were not
right for each other? You may have even said, or thought, "This
marriage won't last." The choice of marriage partner is a very important decision, and whether it turns out to be the right decision
or the wrong decision, it is a decision based on our emotions.

How do we decide on a career? As children and teens we daydream and we fantasize about all sorts of things. This is normal,
natural, and very necessary behavior. We daydream about being a
cowboy, a doctor, an astronaut, a rock star, a movie idol, a police of-
ficer, a schoolteacher, a scientist. By doing this we rule things in
and we rule things out. We start to make decisions about the kinds
of things we would or would not enjoy. We begin making decisions
that move us in certain directions, and eventually this leads to career or job choices. It is what makes us happy, or what we project
will make us happy, or what we think will make us feel fulfilled that
we gravitate toward. Even the simple task of looking for a job in
the want ads is based on emotions. We rule out jobs because we
don't think they would make us happy, or we tend to look for jobs
similar to the ones we have held before because they are more
comfortable. Our emotions are dictating our decisions.

Another way of making a career choice is to never put forth the effort to make a choice, or to achieve, or to delay gratification. That also makes a choice by putting extreme limits on our potentials and our possibilities.

Just as our emotions will impact our career choices, they also will cause us to make changes. How many people have left a job or changed careers because they were not happy, because they did not feel fulfilled, because they did not like their boss or fellow workers? Certainly people will also make choices to change jobs or careers because of cognitive reasons. Not making enough money and needing better insurance coverage are examples of this. But many if not most of the career or job changes we make are based on emotional factors.

Another emotional decision is where people choose to retire. Some will retire right where they have lived because they have friends and family nearby, and they believe they will be happier remaining where they are. Others opt to move somewhere where they can be around people of their own age, or where they can play golf or go fishing every day. Sometimes these are right decisions for them, and sometimes they are wrong, but the point is they are based on emotional needs or projected emotional needs.

What about the discipline problems seen in the office at a middle school or high school? Two boys get into a fight because a girl just dumped one of them and is now going out with the other. There is jealousy, anger, loss, and resentment, and the boys get into trouble because of decisions based on emotional factors. What about the students who get into trouble for drug use? Some students use drugs to feel good. Others use drugs to mask pain. Still others use drugs to feel a part of the group, to fit in. All of these decisions to use drugs are based on emotional factors . . . emotional reasons. Most if not all of the behaviors that get students into trouble and sent to the office at school are because of decisions made that are based on the emotions of the students involved.

Emotions, and the inability to understand and control them, are the main reasons we have student discipline issues. Typically in schools we try to manage behaviors. That is an ongoing proposition because it does not address the real problem. It's like the old joke of the man who goes to the doctor, moves his arm a certain way, and says, "It hurts when I do that." The doctor replies, "Then don't do that." That may take care of the pain, but it does not solve the problem. If we could teach students to better manage emotions, the behavior problems would diminish. Basically, if all students had a higher level of emotional intelligence, school discipline issues would drop significantly.

Let's get a little closer to home. What are you doing Saturday night? Certainly there are times we have responsibilities we must carry out, commitments to family or friends, a dinner or wedding that we may or may not be thrilled about attending, but most of the time we opt to spend Friday or Saturday night doing things we like. We do things that are fun. We do things that make us feel good, that give us pleasure, that are satisfying. Or at least we make plans that we think will accomplish those goals. So what are we really doing? We are making decisions about how we spend the most precious hours we have based on our emotions or on our emotional projections—on how we feel or on how we project what we propose to do will make us feel. Emotions are the key driving force in the decisions we make regarding our free time.

Feelings of commitment and loyalty, feelings of regret or anticipated regret, feelings of guilt or anger play significant roles in the decisions we make. They are very powerful influences in our day-to-day, moment-to-moment decisions. They spur us into action, or they stop us dead in our tracks.

Additionally, let's consider motivation. What is motivation? Where does motivation come from? When we think of the brain and its functioning, we typically think of it as the organ that thinks, that problem solves, that decides what actions to take. That is all true, but what motivates us to take those actions once the decision has been made? What motivates us is loving something, getting excited over something, feeling committed to something, or possibly fearing something. It is these emotions that cause us to get out of bed in the morning and do something. It is these emotions that cause us to accomplish and be accomplished.

The star basketball player doesn't become a star only because she has athletic ability. The star basketball player becomes the star because she loves the game, can't get enough of the excitement of watching that ball go through the net, or loves the praise and esteem gained from being the star. The same is true of the star tennis player or the first-chair violin in the orchestra. The same is true of the honor student. It is emotion that drives the motivation. It is emotion that is the basis for accomplishment and achievement.

Conversely, without emotions there is no motivation. If you can't get a student to love something, to get excited about something, or at least to fear the consequences of not performing to some level, then you won't get much out of him. That is part of the art of teaching, to be able to get students excited and turned on to a project. If you can do that, the student will be motivated. If you deal with students who have emotional problems of one sort or another, notice how often they also have problems with motivation.

The bottom line in looking at the impact, the influence, or the interconnection between emotions and the decisions we make is that emotions are the key. Emotions, understanding emotions, emotional intelligence is not just some gushy-wushy feel-good talk. The big decisions we make in life, the moment-to-moment decisions we make every day, and the motivation to carry out these decisions are all tightly interwoven with our emotional makeup. It is time we start to understand this and to use this in helping our children make decisions, all kinds of decisions, including decisions about bullying and victimization.

CHAPTER SUMMARY/ISSUES

1. Emotions are critical in the decisions we make throughout life, and hence it is critical to develop emotional intelligence as early in life as possible.

2. Emotions are critical in the big decisions we make such as whom to marry, what career to choose, why we leave or change jobs, and even where we retire.

3. Emotions are the driving force behind the decisions teenagers make that land them in trouble.

4. Emotions determine how we choose to spend our time, how we relax, the fun we choose.

5. Emotions are the basis of motivation. We are motivated by what we love and what excites us. There is no motivation without emotions.

6. Children and teens with emotional problems will also typically exhibit motivational problems.

7. Understanding and dealing with emotions is not just a gushy-wushy, feel-good endeavor. Emotions and emotional intelligence are critical in every decision we make, any motivation we have, and hence what we do with our lives.

8

IMPACT BIAS

There was once an old mule that stumbled and fell into a dried-up well. The farmer heard the mule braying and found the mule deep in the well. The farmer thought and thought about how he could get the mule out, but could come up with no solutions. Eventually he made a decision and began hauling loads of dirt to the well. He decided to bury the mule to put it out of its misery. Shovel full by shovel full he threw dirt into the well. The mule became hysterical as it realized what was happening. But then a thought struck the mule. Every time a shovel full of dirt landed on the mule's back it would shrug it off and step up. The mule did this blow after blow, shovel full after shovel full. It would shrug it off and take the next step. After what seemed an eternity, battered and exhausted, the mule stepped triumphantly over the wall of the well and onto the ground. What seemed like a situation that would bury the mule eventually became the manner of the mule's salvation. Out of adversity came the potential for hope and deliverance.

—Unknown

IMPACT BIAS DEFINED

Impact bias, which is a term used by Dr. Daniel Gilbert (2002) of Harvard University, is defined as the bias we have regarding the significance and gravity of events or imminent events in our lives. In other words, when an event occurs in our lives or there is a possibility that an event could occur in our lives, we tend to place greater significance on the result that it will have in our lives than is usually accurate. We overestimate the impact. We blow it out of proportion. We fear that if this certain thing happens it will spell our doom. Or we put all our eggs in one basket, all our hopes that a single event will make our lives complete and we will live happily ever after. Impact bias is our worst nightmare or our greatest fairy tale.

We can see impact bias working in lots of ways. Some of the irrational fears we have are due to impact bias. One of the greatest fears people have is speaking in front of a group. In reality, there is not a lot of bad stuff that can happen as a result of speaking in front of a group. We aren't likely to be cast out of society, destined to live out our lives in a cave, and stoning a speaker is definitely outdated in our society. The worst that might happen is ridicule. Even that is unlikely because most of us feel empathy for a speaker and feel compassion when he or she messes up. Nevertheless, we blow public speaking so out of proportion that most people not only panic at the thought of it, but will not do it under any circumstances.

Dr. Gilbert has done multiple studies regarding impact bias. One study he reported on concerned college professors who were up for tenure. The professors were all asked what it would mean for them if they got tenure, and what it would mean if they did not get tenure. Basically, the professors all stated the same thing. Getting tenure was the be-all and end-all of what they were after. If they got tenure they would be set for life. It would solve all their problems. There would be no more worries. On the other hand, if they did not get tenure it would be devastating. Their plans would be ruined. They would have to rethink their future . . . their lives. It would be a life-changing catastrophe. Possibly that is a little ex- aggerated, but that was the gist of their thinking.

After tenure decisions were made, the researchers went back to these same professors. Some of them had received tenure, and some had not. Those that received tenure were asked if it was all they thought it would be. Basically, these professors stated it was not all they had imagined. There were still issues, concerns, and worries. It did not solve all their problems. It was not the be-all and end-all. Likewise, those professors who did not get tenure were not nearly as upset as they thought they would be. They were coping with it. They were dealing with it. In some cases it had opened up other avenues that were at least equally if not more rewarding. It was not the end of the world. These professors were not jumping off rooftops in droves.

The point is, impact bias is that part of us that makes us fear the worst or expect happily-ever-after results. Impact bias makes us believe that if a feared event happens in our lives, the sun may not come up tomorrow.

THE PSYCHOLOGICAL IMMUNE SYSTEM

But the sun will come up tomorrow, and it is because we have a psychological immune system. Our psychological immune system helps us rationalize and deal with these bad events. It is there within us, but we do not realize just how potent it is. We underes- timate its power.

The psychological immune system is not the same thing as emo- tional intelligence, but it is definitely based on emotional intelli- gence. The higher the level of one's emotional intelligence, the healthier one's psychological immune system. This makes sense if we think about it. The more tools and the better tools we have emotionally, the better we will be able to do the job of managing or coping with major catastrophes or setbacks in our lives.

A key point here is that we all have impact bias, but we all have varying levels of a psychological immune system. Some people have much healthier psychological immune systems than others. Teenagers are certainly victims of impact bias, but since the psychological immune system is based on emotional intelligence, and since teenagers are lower on the continuum of emotional intelligence, they do not typically have as healthy a psychological immune system. This means they do not and will not cope with things as well as they would if the same events happened to them later on in their lives. This is why teenagers are so quick to commit suicide. This is why teenagers will get a gun and bring it to school to get even. This is why teenagers are so easily goaded into fights. This is why teenagers will run away from home or will get into drugs to escape. Teenagers are, for the most part, very emotional creatures. They are easily manipulated emotionally. They will become enraged, dismayed, or passionate about a cause or an injustice. Emotional appeals are potent with teenagers. This is all because they have a psychological immune system that is immature, which translates into the fact that they do not cope with, rationalize, or manage emotional information and issues well.

This is another powerful reason to model and teach emotional intelligence. Besides being a means to decrease bullying and the impact of bullying, it is a means to protect our children from poor decisions ending in suicide, homicide, drug use, or a variety of other dangerous and harmful behaviors.

HOW THE PSYCHOLOGICAL IMMUNE SYSTEM WORKS

Dr. Gilbert reports on some interesting studies that demonstrate how our psychological immune system really works in our lives. One study he reported on was done with Harvard students. Some students were offered the opportunity to learn black-and-white photography. They were provided with a camera and film. They were taught how to work the cameras, how to select good photo possibilities, how to set up the shots, how to use natural lighting, and so on. Then they were sent out to take photos. After taking the photos they were taught how to develop their shots, and then they were asked to select their two favorite photos. These were developed into 8 × 10 glossy prints. Then they were asked to select which photo they would like to keep. The students, up until that point, had thought they would get to keep both photos, but now they were told they got to keep only one. The other photo was needed to send to the home office to show what the project was accomplishing.

Here is where the study came in. Half the students were told to make their decisions immediately because the photo they did not select was being placed in the mail at that moment to be shipped to the home office. In other words, their decision was final. The other half of the students were asked to make a decision right then, but they were told that the other photo was not going to be sent off until this time next week. If they wanted to change their minds about which photo they wanted to keep, they could come back and the photos would be switched . . . no questions asked. In fact, they could change their minds as often as they liked. They could switch photos every day until next week if they wanted. In other words, their decisions were not final; they could change their minds.

Ultimately, all photos were shipped and all decisions were final. Then the researchers went back to all the students in the project and asked them how happy they were with the decision they made. Those students who had been forced to make an immediate decision and stick with it were all happy with their choices. A decision had to be made, they had made it, and their psychological immune systems were kicking in and helping them rationalize their choice. Those who could change their minds, and some of them did several times, were never satisfied with their decisions. They could have changed their minds. They had that option. They could have had the other one. They were tormented. They were doubting themselves. This group couldn't rationalize their decisions as easily because they could have made a different decision.

Sometimes we may think we are being kind and benevolent if we give teens the chance to change their minds about issues, but psychologically it may be better for them, healthier for them, if we insist that they live with the choices they make.

This is similar to other issues we face in life. Those issues that go on and on and we can't get resolved are often harder on us than events that occur but have an ending, a culmination to them . . . no matter how devastating the end result might be. For example, as devastating to a teenager as the death of a parent might be, it is often harder on a teenager to watch the imminent death of a parent who lingers near death for years. The death can be grieved. The prolonged dying is suffered but cannot be grieved until there is a finalization to it.

Another study that Dr. Gilbert discusses demonstrates how the psychological immune system helps us live with decisions. In this study each subject was to look at six Monet prints and align them in order of their personal preference. Their favorite was to be number one and their least favorite number six. After each subject had made his or her decisions, the researchers always made a statement such as "It just so happens that we have extra prints of the ones you selected as numbers three and four, the ones right in the middle. We will give you a copy of the one you selected as number three as a thank-you for participating in this project. However, since the prints you selected as numbers three and four are obviously close in your ranking, please look at those two again and see if you are happy with them or if you care to switch number four with number three." Some subjects did switch four with three and some did not, but eventually everyone went home with a print of the one they had put in the third position (i.e., the print they liked third best in this group).

A month later all the subjects were brought back and asked to again lay the prints out in order of preference. They were told this was not a memory test; they were not being asked to lay them out as they had laid them out before. They were told, in fact, that people change their minds over time, and the researchers wanted to see if they had changed their minds. Therefore, they were given the same instructions, to lay out the prints one through six in order of their preference. The results were interesting. In every case the print the subject had selected as number three in the first round, the one they had taken home, always went up in their esteem to the number one or two position. And the print they had selected as number four, which had been close to their third choice in the first round, always moved down in their esteem to the number five or six position. It could be argued that since they were regularly looking at the one they had taken home, it could have grown on them and hence they liked it better, but that would not explain why number four also dropped in their esteem. It is very interesting how the psychological immune system kicks in to help people rationalize that they made the right choice.

It is also interesting that this exact project was done with people who had memory problems. When they were brought back for the second time, they were asked if they remembered which prints they had selected as numbers three and four. These subjects could not remember. The researchers stated that was all right, this was not a memory test, would they please lay out the prints in order of their preference as of this moment. The results were exactly the same as with all the other subjects. The print they had gone home with, even though these subjects could not remember which one that was, always moved up to the one or two position. Likewise, the one they had selected as number four in the first round always moved down in their esteem to number five or six. Even though their cognitive memory was not functioning, their psychological immune system was functioning quite well.

A third study demonstrated how the psychological immune system can be impacted. In this study, which was again done with Harvard students, a job opportunity was posted. The job was to work for a new ice cream company and taste new flavors. After tasting the flavors, those hired would be asked to help name the new flavors. The hourly rate for this job was also made appealing. (It sounds like a job I would apply for right now.) At any rate, there were lots of applicants. Each applicant had to go through an interview. Each applicant was also told that the person or persons making the hiring decisions wanted to remain anonymous for personal reasons. That person, or persons, were behind a two-way mirror and would be watching the interview. Half of the applicants were told there was one person behind the mirror, and the other half were told there was a panel of six people behind the mirror making the decision. These applicants were also told, however, that if any one of the six people behind the mirror liked them, then they would get the job. In other words, all six people on the panel would have to veto the applicant in order to not get hired. All applicants were then interviewed, and each one was told in turn, "Sorry, you don't get the job."

Shortly after the interview and again days later, each was asked how he or she felt about not getting hired. Those who thought that one person had turned them down were handling it well. Their psychological immune systems were kicking in and helping them cope. They stated such things as "That person made a mistake. I would have done a good job," or "Possibly I did something that reminded them of someone they don't like," or "Maybe my first name is the same as someone they don't like." The point is, they were coping, they were fine. Those who thought they were turned down by six people, on the other hand, were really struggling. They were making comments such as "What's wrong with me?" "How am I presenting myself?" "What did I do wrong?" "How can I improve?"

Notice the difference in focus. Those rejected by a group focused comments on themselves, while those rejected by one person were not focused on themselves. This is a significant point. If we want to change someone's attitude toward something, having a group give the message is much more potent than an individual giving the message. In therapy, for example, a group that works well and gives an individual member a consistent message will have much more impact on that individual than if an individual therapist gives the message. Individual therapy can be effective in helping someone change who wants to change and needs help doing so, but to change an individual's attitude about an issue is much more powerful through a group. One individual's ideas can be blown off too easily. If a group is saying something, it is not nearly as easy to disregard. This is another reason why the message about bullying needs to get out to all students . . . so that the group, the milieu at school, is antibullying.

CHAPTER SUMMARY/ISSUES

1. Impact bias is the weight, or the impact, we believe events will have in our lives. We all tend to overestimate the impact events will have.
2. The psychological immune system, which is highly dependent on emotional intelligence, is what helps us rationalize or cope with issues and events in our lives.
3. The psychological immune system moderates impact bias.
4. Teenagers are also affected by impact bias, but they have a lesser developed psychological immune system. This is why teenagers will so readily make decisions to commit suicide, bring a gun to school to get even, get involved with drugs and alcohol, run away, and so on.
5. Our psychological immune system helps us cope with the decisions and choices we make.
6. Although it may seem very benevolent to allow teens to change their minds about choices they have made, doing so instills doubt and actually makes it harder for them to rationalize and cope with their decisions.

7. It is ultimately easier to deal with the reality and finality of an event than the turmoil and uncertainty of an ongoing, prolonged situation.

8. The psychological immune system can be impacted more strongly and severely by a group than by mere individuals. Hence, having a school milieu that is antibullying will have far greater impact than one-on-one interventions with bullies.

THE LIMBIC SYSTEM

I took a piece of plastic clay
And idly fashioned it one day.
And as my fingers pressed it, still,
It moved and yielded to my will.

I came again, when days were passed,
That bit of clay was hard at last.
The form I gave it, still it bore,
And I could change that form no more.

Then I took a piece of living clay
And gently formed it day by day
And molded with my power and art
A young child's soft and yielding heart.

I came again when years were gone.
It was a man I looked upon.
He still that early impress bore,
And I could change it nevermore.

—Unknown

THE SEAT OF EMOTIONS

The amygdala, which is a part of the deep limbic system, is the seat of emotions. Emotionally charged memories, good and bad, are stored here. This includes trauma. The limbic system is where events that happen in our lives are coded as significant, as emotional, and thus this gives emotional overtones to our thoughts and our outlook. The limbic system is where love and bonding and the ability to form connections are located. The limbic system also directly processes the sense of smell. The sense of smell is the only one of the five sensory systems that goes directly from the sense organ to the area of the brain that processes it. All other systems are channeled through a relay station of sorts. The sense of smell, however, is crucial in the immediate recognition of danger.

The fact that the sense of smell is processed in the limbic system explains why smell has such an impact on our emotions. Why is the perfume industry in existence? And when a man presents his lady with flowers, yes, they are pretty, but they also smell wonderful and create an immediate emotional response. The limbic system, as mentioned earlier in this book, also modulates motivation. Without emotion there will be no motivation. Fear and anxiety responses are located in the limbic system. Fight-or-flight responses are triggered from the limbic system. The limbic system is not a separate, isolated system, however. It is connected to all other parts of the brain. Hence, feelings of fear and anxiety can hijack our thoughts and functioning.

ROUTINE

There are many examples of how fear, anxiety, or other powerful emotions hijack our thoughts and reasoning abilities. A perfect example of this can be seen in the sport of golf. If you have ever participated in competitive golf, or watched people who do so, you have undoubtedly seen some of the contestants fall apart. The anxiety of competition causes some people to not be able to perform as they are capable of performing. In qualifications for any city golf championship, there will be those golfers who have the skills to play in the championship flight but who will inevitably become so anxious that they will mishit shots, jerk shots left, push shots right, look up on shots and top the ball, and miss short putts. As the mistakes mount the anxiety grows. This happens routinely in amateur golf competitions.

This can also be seen at the professional level, but not as often. One reason for this, and it is not merely because of the skill level, is that many professional golfers have sports psychologists counseling them on how to handle their emotions so they don't fall apart. Sports psychologists tell them to do calming exercises such as taking deep breaths, focusing on pleasant memories or pleasant outcomes, imagining the shot played perfectly in their minds, and developing a routine before every shot. These kinds of activities are very helpful in getting a golfer past the anxiety and allowing her to execute the shot as she has learned to execute it. But what is really going on? The advice is great, but until recently it was not really understood why it worked or what it did in the brain.

In this chapter we have identified the limbic system as the seat of emotions. When you are anxious your limbic system is in charge . . . it is prepared to give your body orders involving fight or flight. Earlier in this book we discussed how novel thoughts and responses are located in the right hemisphere of the brain, and routine functions shift to and are located in the left hemisphere of the brain. Utilizing a routine before each shot is designed to actually shift the locus of control in the brain to the left hemisphere. If we can shift which part of the brain is actually in control at a particular moment, and move it at will to the left hemisphere, we can execute the shot that we have learned and practiced executing.

We can see the same thing in basketball. Good free-throw shooters go through a very specific routine before every free throw they take. This routine settles them. In reality, it allows the left hemisphere in their brains to take over.

Have you ever noticed baseball players in their prebatting routine? Watch the way a player will unwrap and wrap his gloves. How he will move his bat. The wiggles and squirms he makes. He will do the same thing every time. Why? It appears as though baseball players are the most superstitious people in the world, the way they cross themselves, kiss their necklaces, tap their shoulders, tap the ground, point their bats, and on and on. They may be superstitious, but the point is they perform better when they go through these gyrations. The reason they do perform better is not that their routine movements have a mystical power; it's that the routine settles them. The routine shifts the locus of control into the left hemisphere and allows them to function as they have taught their bodies to function.

What about military or police training? Soldiers and police officers are trained relentlessly on how to respond in crisis situations. It is crucial that they are trained. A potentially life or death situation is emotionally charged. You cannot expect individuals to think their way through a situation when they could be in crisis. Their responses must be practiced, drilled into them, routine . . . so that the routine can take over. This not only keeps them from making critical mistakes but also empowers them to act quickly and decisively. This training is crucial because if you have ever been in a crisis, you know that you cannot think your way through it. At that point your emotions are starting to take over.

Another example can be seen in dealing with children who have autism. If you have ever worked with young autistic children, you know that they desperately need structure and routine. If the routine they have or the structure they expect is not there, they will immediately go into fight-or-flight mode. They may tantrum, run, or lash out. If you have ever had to chase a child who ran out the door because the normal routine was disrupted, you understand this perfectly. Routine is calming for most children because it helps them remain in the left hemisphere of the brain. When routine and structure are not there, a child's emotions may take over and the limbic system dictates fight or flight.

What about meditation? For centuries the art of meditation has been practiced in the Far East. Fairly recently it has become more common in our culture. Meditation is the art of altering mental states. By doing so one can lower one's pulse rate, breathing rate, metabolism, and so forth. What really is happening in meditation is that the individual moves almost all voluntary brain activity from the limbic system and from the right hemisphere to the left hemisphere. This is done through a variety of methods, all of which develop and utilize routine and systematically move the person into a routine state of mind. Some methods involve using a mantra such as "ohm," or using a method of focused breathing in and out, or using a method of repeatedly counting breaths slowly to 10. All of the relaxation methods involve repetition and routine, and they can have significant health and mental health benefits. The significant factor to note here is that meditation is used as a method of shifting the locus of control in the brain.

Another example is sleep or sleep problems. Have you ever been unable to sleep because you were upset emotionally? Because you were distraught, tense, angry, hurt, jealous, or afraid? Or have you ever been unable to sleep because you had a problem on your mind and you were trying to work out a solution and you just couldn't let it go? The standard solutions to attain sleep include counting sheep, focusing on breathing in and out, and focusing on relaxing the body one part at a time. These are all methods of moving the locus of control of the brain out of the limbic system if you're upset, or out of the right hemisphere if you're in problem-solving mode, and into the left hemisphere so you can let your body do what it needs to do.

All these examples are things we see or do daily, and they all involve shifting the locus of control temporarily to the left hemisphere. We can learn to do this. We can be taught to do this. People with more advanced levels of emotional intelligence recognize the importance of this and find ways to do it. Golfers and athletes of all kinds try to find ways to calm themselves so they can perform. Musicians, actors, and orators try to find ways of lowering performance anxiety. Every day people recognize that high anxiety is not good for them and attempt to calm themselves in various ways. Understanding that what we are really doing is shifting the locus of control to the left hemisphere of the brain is monumental. Once we understand this, we can be more decisive about how to most successfully achieve that. We can also utilize this in dealing with children to help them achieve the ability to intentionally make such a shift in the locus of control of brain activity.

GRIEF, TRAUMA, AND STORIES

There is a difference between grief and trauma. Mental health professionals know this. Grief is a process of healing from an unsettling event such as a major loss. Trauma is being stuck in that event. For someone in grief, getting him to talk about his emotions may be very helpful. For someone in trauma, however, attempts to get her to talk about what she is feeling are often unsuccessful.

Cheri Lovre (2004), who is a specialist in grief, trauma, and crisis management, gives a wonderful example of managing trauma. To the best of my recollection, the story goes something like this. A woman was in trauma because her daughter had been shot to death. The woman had tried counseling, but it had not helped. Every thought she had of her daughter went straight to the memory of her daughter's brutal murder. The woman was having nightmares on a regular basis. The nightmare was always the same. She would see her daughter standing there, she would see the gunman pointing the gun, and just as he pulled the trigger, the woman would wake up in heart-pounding panic. She was stuck in the trauma. Attempts to get her to talk about what she was feeling could not get her past the trauma. She could not talk about the event without reexperiencing the horror.

What eventually worked for her was when she was asked to tell the story of her daughter's life. Telling the story of her daughter's life put the brutal murder in perspective. It was a piece of her daughter's story. But the factor of utmost importance here is that telling the story of her daughter's life put her life into language. Telling the story took some of the pain that was locked in the limbic system, where emotionally charged memories are stored, and moved it to the left hemisphere, where, in adults, language is controlled or regulated. This shift was enough that it made a dramatic change.

That night the woman again had the dream, only it did not stop at the point of the actual shooting. This time it continued. The daughter was shot, the woman went to her daughter's side, she took her daughter's hand, and she told her daughter that she loved her and would miss her. The next day she began to grieve. The story allowed her to shift the locus of control, to grieve, to unblock the trauma. It allowed her to remember the good and the bad memories she had of her daughter. It allowed her to laugh, and cry, and love. Every thought of her daughter did not go straight to the shooting. This is powerful. The concept that we can unblock trauma by utilizing stories and hence language to shift the locus of control from one part of the brain to another is of indescribable value.

Another example of the power of utilizing stories and language can be found in the use of social stories with special education students. This social story technique involves telling and writing down routines and agendas so that the child can comprehend what has happened or will happen. The teacher or staff member will take pencil and paper and do the writing, but the child becomes engaged in telling the story of the event. It's his story. He is the main character, and this hooks him into the telling of it. The significance, however, is that putting the story into language both establishes routine and moves the event out of the limbic system and into the parts of the brain that control language and routine. These children have to be taught the process of social stories, but once they have been taught, this intervention will calm them when nothing else will. It is effective because it shifts the locus of control in the brain.

Storytelling is a very powerful tool with young children in dealing with all sorts of issues. Up until the age of roughly 11 or 12, counseling is not very effective with children because they cannot sit down and discuss their issues and grasp the rationale of why this works and that doesn't work. Stories work well, however, because children can identify with the characters and learn from that identification. Basically this is modeling behavior through the characters. However, when children are upset or traumatized by an event, the use of the right stories can calm them, not only because it models behavior but also because it utilizes language that can move the trauma they are having out of the emotional center, the limbic system, and into a different part of the brain. Again, utilizing what we now understand of brain function can be a wonderful tool for counseling and calming.

PLAY VERSUS LIFE AND DEATH

A number of different types of situations were mentioned earlier that involve shifting the locus of control from the limbic system to the left hemisphere in the brain. This is very useful in sports such as golf. When a golfer is in a competitive situation and lets the anxiety and stress take over instead of understanding how to utilize the power of shifting the locus of control to his left hemisphere, he can literally fall apart. He can become so anxious that he cannot swing the club properly, and every mistake seems to make the problem worse. The stress builds and the result is frustration and humiliation. People have given up the game of golf because of such episodes.

But the golfer who shoots poorly because of the anxiety of competition can go back out the next day when he is not competing and his golf swing will return. When the stress is gone he can again function. The point is, golf is only a game . . . it is not a life or death situation. You would think that anxiety and stress would not take this kind of toll on something that is, in the long run, so trivial. But it does.

Now think about the teenager who is facing a stressful, anxiety-producing event. Add in the factor of impact bias so that she believes the event will be even more life changing, life altering, life shattering than an adult would know it would be, and it becomes easy to understand how fear and anxiety can supplant clear and logical reasoning. It becomes easy to understand how and why teenagers will make decisions that result in such severe consequences. They will commit suicide, bring a gun to school to get even, get into fights, get involved with drugs, run away, go into deep depressions. Situations such as the shootings at Columbine and Thurston High School were perpetrated by children who were experiencing anger, hurt, anxiety, stress, rage, humiliation, and who knows what else. Teaching children and teenagers some of the ways of shifting into the left hemisphere of the brain, why this is important, and how it can help them can be of tremendous benefit for them.

STRESS

Stress has been mentioned in various cases, but we should focus specifically on stress for a moment. There are four conditions that can evoke stress:

1. Novelty
2. Unpredictability
3. Low sense of control
4. Threat to the ego

In stressful situations the body releases a glucocorticoid called cortisol, which is a neurotransmitter. At the same time the body inhibits the release of serotonin, a neurotransmitter that relaxes and calms one's mind. The combination of the increased cortisol and decreased serotonin in the brain induces the infamous fight-or-flight response. This is a necessary lifesaving response. Faced with a dangerous situation, it may be necessary to fight or flee to save our lives. Sometimes the most critical part is in knowing when to fight and when to flee, but that's another issue. The key is that this is a necessary part of our ability to protect ourselves. However, continued stress and continued high levels of cortisol are very damaging.

The hippocampus, which is part of the limbic system and very necessary for monitoring stress and emotional memory, has receptors for cortisol. Sonia Lupien (2004) reports on studies done with posttraumatic stress disorder (PTSD) patients coming back from war. What they have found is that the hippocampus is decreased in volume, up to a 13% or more reduction. This was considered to be the result of high levels of cortisol over extended periods of time, causing a deterioration of the hippocampus, a sort of wear and tear theory of how the hippocampus gets depleted. More recent studies have also looked at siblings and even twins of some of these PTSD soldiers. What has been found is that the hippocampus of these siblings is also depleted even though they did not go to war and are not PTSD patients. Some researchers are now thinking that it is stress in children, with continued high levels of cortisol, that causes the hippocampus not to develop to the expected volume. Later, when faced with high levels of stress and lacking the normal volume of hippocampus to effectively manage stress, the individual develops PTSD. In other words, it is not the high levels of cortisol in stressed adults that depletes the hippocampus, but rather high levels of cortisol in stressed children that keeps the hippocampus from developing. This has not yet been proven, but it appears to be the only way to account for the low hippocampus level in siblings of PTSD patients.

What causes stress in children? One key answer is poverty. Studies have shown that children living in poverty have higher blood pressure than children not in poverty. High blood pressure is a key indicator of stress. Look at the conditions of stress. Novelty—children in poverty tend to move around a great deal, and the family makeup changes much more often. Unpredictability—children in poverty often don't know how long they will be living in their current home or how long they will be attending their current school. Low sense of control—children in poverty do not have control over their situations, and furthermore, studies have shown that children who are not in poverty tend to believe that anything is possible, while children in poverty do not believe that. Threat to ego—children in poverty tend to perform poorly in school compared with other students, not because they are less capable but because of a variety of other influencing factors. This, however, is interpreted as being less intelligent and less capable, thus affecting the ego.

Other situations also cause continued stress in children. Living in a situation of domestic violence or living with abuse and neglect can certainly cause stress. Being the victim of bullying on a regular basis is also a key contributor to stress. A child does not have to be bullied every day to feel stress. If a child is bullied even periodically, she will fear it every day and the stress will be present every day. Hence, allowing children to be bullied is possibly impacting brain development by causing the hippocampus not to develop to its normal growth, which in turn decreases the victim's ability to manage stress later on in life.

THE SIGNIFICANCE OF SMELL

Odors can be pleasant or unpleasant, but beyond that many people generally attach no significance to what they smell. However, we need to rethink that. Why is it that the sense of smell is processed in the limbic system . . . the system that controls and dictates emotional response? The fact is, odor is very crucial in determining such things as danger or recognition. Odor can tell us when there is smoke in the air and the house is on fire. Odor can tell us when something is rancid and we should throw it out instead of eat it. Odor can trigger the fight-or-flight response immediately when danger lurks. Odor can help the mother recognize her young, and the infant recognize the mother. Odor is designed to trigger immediate responses, and it very significantly can impact our actions and our behaviors.

An interesting experiment was done by Wedekind, Seebeck, Bettens, and Paepke (1995). He had male college students wear T-shirts long enough to get their odors on the shirts. He then had female college students smell the shirts and rank them in order of preference (i.e., the scents they liked versus the ones they did not like). He also did genetic tests on all the students involved. What he found was that the female students were more drawn to the odors of students who were more genetically different from themselves. This makes sense biologically. It would be disastrous if we were drawn to—if we found appealing—the odors of our brothers and sisters. Genetically we are set up not to find our siblings attractive. This helps us have offspring that are healthier, because when we have DNA from two people mixing to develop a child, and there are similar defects in the DNA, the child will more readily have a genetic problem. If two people with different DNA couple, and one of them has a gene that is defective, the healthy gene from the other partner will also be passed along, and the child has a chance of being healthy. In this way, odor works to protect us and promote healthy offspring.

Wedekind's research also found that the selection process— what was appealing or what was not appealing—was thrown off in the female students who took birth control pills. The process was random. In other words, these students were attracted to odors that were not necessarily different genetically. Does this mean that the use of birth control pills has possibly had an unintended impact on our society and has caused people who would not normally have been attracted to each other to actually be attracted to each other, possibly having offspring with genetic issues? Is it possible that some of the learning disabilities, autism, and so on have indirectly resulted from the use of birth control pills? That is not the point of this discussion, but what is significant is that odor has a more important role in our lives than we realize.

There are odors that evoke negative responses from students, and there are odors that evoke more positive responses from students. Some students are natural victims of bullying and harassment because they smell bad. Can we do something about that? Most certainly. Additionally, students who tend to be aggressive and violent toward others can be influenced and calmed with pleasant odors. Odor is certainly not the most important factor in dealing with the bullying issue, but it can be a factor and in some cases is a significant factor. It should be a consideration if nothing else.

CHAPTER SUMMARY/ISSUES

1. The limbic system is the seat of emotions.
2. The limbic system processes the sense of smell.
3. The limbic system is tied to all other parts of the brain, which is why emotions can hijack our thoughts and behaviors.
4. Sports offer a great example of how fear and anxiety can interfere with an athlete's ability to perform.
5. Establishing routine is the solution to managing performance anxiety.
6. Routine processes are generally located in the left hemisphere of the brain.
7. Getting into established routines automatically shifts the locus of control in the brain from the limbic system, where anxiety may be rampant, to the left hemisphere, where routine is monitored.
8. Military and police training pointedly establish routines for dealing with crisis situations.
9. People who work with young children, especially those with autism, know how crucial it is to maintain structure and routine in their day. Without it, children tend to panic and lose control.

10. Meditation and sleep problems are examples of how utilizing routine can shift the locus of control and have a calming, relaxing effect.

11. Establishing routines can be used with victims of bullying to calm them and give them some control over their responses.

12. Grief is a natural and healing response to an event of loss, while trauma is being stuck in the event.

13. Putting traumatic memories into words, into stories, into language can help shift the trauma out of the limbic system and into the left hemisphere where language is processed. This can move the event from trauma to grief.

14. Social stories are techniques used to help provide children with information, which is calming. This technique utilizes language to shift the locus of control and help the child regain or maintain inner control. Children with autism often respond well to social stories.

15. Storytelling in general can be a powerful tool in calming children or individuals of all ages.

16. While anxiety can so easily take over in sports performances, these are not life or death situations. They are relatively meaningless. A teenager facing a stressful situation, with the added elements of impact bias and the lack of a fully functional psychological immune system, is another story. This explains why teens can so quickly make poor decisions resulting in suicide, running away, getting involved with drugs, or bringing a gun to school to get even.

17. The four conditions of stress are novelty, unpredictability, low sense of control, and threat to ego.

18. Stress causes the body to release cortisol, which initiates the fight-or-flight response.

19. The hippocampus has receptors for cortisol.

20. It has long been thought that continued stress, and hence continued high levels of cortisol in the system, actually wear away the hippocampus, sometimes resulting in posttraumatic stress disorder.

21. It may be that it is stress in childhood, and the resulting high levels of cortisol, that actually keep the hippocampus from developing to its normal volume.

22. Poverty, domestic violence, child abuse and neglect, and continued victimization from a bully all create stress in children.

23. These stressors may well be impacting brain development and sentencing the stressed individuals to decreased capability of managing stress effectively as adults.

24. Odor is processed in the limbic system because it is so clearly related to safety and emotions.

25. Odor can trigger immediate fear and hence the fight-or-flight response.

26. We are also attracted by odors, and this helps the mother and baby identify each other, as well as affects attraction to the opposite sex.

27. Odors can even play a part in victimization, and their importance cannot be overlooked.

⑩

THE CONNECTIONS THAT BIND US

These two science teachers had become friends. One Saturday afternoon they were taking a walk through the countryside enjoying the day and looking for ideas for classroom projects. They took a shortcut through a field and came upon a deep hole.

"I wonder how deep this hole is?" asked one of the teachers.

"Let's see," said the other one, picking up a small pebble and dropping it into the hole. They both listened for the pebble to hit bottom, but heard nothing.

"That wasn't a big enough pebble," said the first. "Find a rock, a big one so we can hear it hit bottom." They looked around and found a rock the size of a fist. They threw it down the hole and listened. Again they heard nothing.

"Not big enough," they agreed. They soon found a rock they had to carry with both hands, lugged it over to the hole and dropped it down. Still nothing. Now they were intrigued over finding the answer to the hole's depth. They searched for something really big, something they knew they would hear when it hit bottom. They came upon a rusty old transmission, dragged it over to the hole and shoved it in. They listened, and heard nothing from the hole, but did hear something behind them. They turned and saw a goat charging toward them. They dove out of the way, the goat missed them, and the goat dove straight down the hole. They were aghast. Then a farmer drove up on his tractor.

"Have you possibly seen my goat?" he asked.

"Yes," they replied. "It charged us, we jumped out of the way, and it dove straight down that hole."

"That's strange," said the farmer. "That goat was chained to a transmission."

—Unknown

THE MOBILITY CRISIS

The connections in our lives are so very much a part of us, so very much who we are. It is not that we merely learn from those connections, which we do. It is not that we are made up of those connections but that we *are* those connections. According to Dr. Thomas Cottle (2004), relationships are not side-by-side experiences . . . they are face-to-face. We are held hostage by those people who have looked us in the eye and loved who we are. It is those relationships, those connections, that make up the person that each of us is. We cannot afford to overlook the significance of connections. Every experience in life changes the neurons in our brains, and connections are indescribably important in making such significant and positive changes.

There are so many things in our society today that detract from or lessen the opportunity to find and build connections. The fact that people move around so much more today than they did several decades ago is one major factor. This results in children changing schools much more often. In fact, in some schools the transient/mobile rate for students is more than 50% of the school population every year. This means that in any given year, more than half of the population of that school will change; half of the population will move out and an entire new half will move in during the school year. Some students will move multiple times during a year. I personally have known elementary school children who moved up to seven times within 1 year. This is not Detroit, Miami, or Houston I'm talking about. This is in the relatively small midwestern town of Bloomington, Indiana.

This high mobility rate takes its toll in schools and on students in a very significant way, and numerous studies have shown this (Fowler-Finn, 2001; Nelson, Simoni, & Adelman, 1996; Stover, 2000). The first major impact of high mobility shows up in academic progress. Students who move frequently have significant gaps in their learning. The transition may mean they go to one school one day and another school the next day, but they lose weeks and weeks in their education with each move. Think about it. The new teacher has to quickly figure out where they are in each subject. What is their reading level? What concepts do they have, and do they lack in mathematics? More significantly, mobile students are stressed. The most significant factor in the students' minds is whether the other students will like them, accept them, not bully them. That is a significant stressor, and until the students resolve that issue at least to some degree, real education takes a backseat.

When a student moves often, this continual starting and stopping takes its toll on motivation. It is hard to continually need to catch up to where the rest of a class is on assignments and projects. Often the mobile student will stop trying to catch up. There is much documentation to prove that mobile students do much more poorly academically and on standardized testing (School Board News, 2002). With the big push on accountability and so much testing being demanded by state and national government entities, it would be worth charting just how differently a school's stable students are doing in relation to those students who move around.

All of the impact that mobility has on students is not in academics, however. Student mobility has a huge impact on behavior. Students who are mobile get sent to the office for disciplinary actions more often than students who are in the stable population group.

This is not typically because they do not know the school rules, although that is sometimes a factor. But school rules tend to be somewhat uniform, and more often offenses are because mobile students choose not to follow the rules. These students do not have the connections with faculty and staff that other students have. When you know someone, when you have a history with someone, what that individual thinks of you is so much more important than what a stranger thinks of you. To the mobile student, especially the student who moved last month and knows she will probably move again in another month or two, these new faculty members are not important . . . they are strangers. Why should the mobile student obey them? Why should the mobile student care what they think? This has a significant impact on behavior.

Mobility also impacts the student's emotional state. True self-esteem comes through achievement, through accomplishment. Since the typical mobile student does not achieve or accomplish at the same level as his less mobile peers, he integrates that into self-perception, and the interpretation is that he has less skill, less ability, less intelligence. Additionally the mobile student is constantly on the outside of social groups trying to work his way inside, to gain acceptance. The combination of these issues is that the mobile student often feels bad about himself, self-esteem is low, there is less sense of worth, there is the tendency to give up, there is little sense of control, and there is often an acceptance of a lower status in the group and hence in life. The result of this can be a wide range of feelings including depression, rejection, alienation, bitterness, or defiance.

The emotional issues tie right in with social issues. The constant state of being put on the outside of social groups and being forced to either try to gain acceptance or merely accept the status of outsider is stressful. The mobile student knows the feelings of isolation, of alienation, of loneliness. The mobile student, who is new to a school and often alone, is an easy target for the class bully. In fact, the mobile student will often be the victim of bullying in one or more of its forms. Conversely, some mobile students have learned to survive by becoming the bully. If the mobile student comes to a new school and bullies other students, she will be safer from being put in the victim role again. The mobile student is often either the victim or the bully.

Motivation is another issue for the mobile student. A lot is expected of these students. The fact that they have less success academically compared with their peers, the fact that they are often on the outside of social groups and always begin at a new school on the outside, the fact that they tend to have lower self-esteem and less confidence in their abilities all tend to negatively impact their motivation. These students come into a new classroom and the teacher expects them to get busy, work hard, try to get caught up—and this is exactly what they have little inclination to do. They may have tried the first time they moved, the second time, the third time, but it becomes harder and harder to find that motivation. Consequently the mobile student will typically put forth less effort than her peers, and the skill gulf widens even further.

Think of the effort it takes to start a new job, to catch up with your fellow workers to learn what you need to know to function adequately and comfortably. This is difficult even if you have good skills. If you don't have good skills, and you are forced into this sort of situation on a regular basis, it becomes very difficult to find that inner motivation to really try.

Each of these issues is significant in and of itself, but the fact is they influence each other and create a downward spiral that has a very negative effect on the student. The mobile student has a far greater likelihood of dropping out or getting expelled from school. This hurts them and this hurts society. The dropout or expelled individual has a far greater chance of getting involved in deviant behavior, getting involved in criminal behavior, getting put on the welfare rolls, or ending up in prison.

Making connections with mobile students is critical. It will impact bullying, and it will impact many other significant issues as well.

NAME-CALLING—IN A GOOD SENSE

Name-calling has a negative connotation. Calling someone by their given name, however, has very positive results. Neuroimaging has shown that when an individual's name is used, the brain is much more highly activated than when the individual's name is not used. Dr. Harvey Silver (2000) has discussed some interesting studies that have been done to show the importance of using a student's name. One study he reports on demonstrates how using the student's name impacts learning. The researchers taped a lesson on audiotape for students. Some students had merely the taped lesson, while some had their names dubbed into the tape throughout. All the students listened to the lesson and were then tested on what they retained. The students who had their names added into the lesson did 4 times better on the posttest. A month later the students were retested for long-term retention, and the discrepancy was even greater. Those students with their names interwoven throughout the lesson forgot significantly less of the information. These students scored 10 times better than their peers long term.

Another study Dr. Silver related concerned a school that made two changes in order to build connections. The first thing they did was to make sure that every morning every student was greeted by name when he or she entered the school. The second change they made was aimed at generating better connections between students. They had students spend the first 15 minutes of every day talking with other students. This was not to hang out with friends but to give students the opportunity to meet with a variety of other students in the school. After a period of time several significant changes were noted. First, attendance rates went up. Second, referrals to the office for fighting and bullying went down. Third, test scores went up. These are all results that schools want, and taking the time to build and encourage connections is a great way to achieve these results.

BONDING

Dr. J. David Hawkins (1993) did an extensive and interesting study several years ago with children living in poor neighborhoods and dangerous environments. He studied students who were making it in school, who were not getting involved with drugs, who were not getting into trouble at school or with the police or the courts, who were being successful in life despite the fact they were growing up in poor neighborhoods and poor environments. What was it that made these children successful while many around them were headed toward self-destruction? He found that there were risk factors and protective factors. Without discussing all of these factors, the number one protective factor was bonding. Every one of these successful students had bonded with a significant adult in his or her life. That adult might have been a parent, someone in the neighborhood, a teacher, a coach, a counselor, a social worker, a janitor, a Big Brother, or a Big Sister, but there was someone. That bonding, that connection, is a crucial element in children's lives. Dr. Edward Hallowell (2002) also discusses building connections in childhood as a critical element in finding happiness as an adult. We could turn so many lives around if we just took the time to make sure that every child has the opportunity to build connections.

CHAPTER SUMMARY/ISSUES

1. Connections are what make us who we are.
2. Today's fast-paced, transient society works against people building connections.
3. Transiency/mobility among students takes a significant toll on them.
4. Transiency often creates both victims and bullies.
5. Transiency impacts students academically, behaviorally, emotionally, socially, and motivationally.

6. These issues are each in themselves significant, but they also interact with each other, causing a downward spiral for the transient student.

7. Calling a student by name creates positive connections, the impact of which can be noted in the brain through neuro-imaging.

8. Having students spend time getting to know other students in a school has a positive impact in multiple ways.

9. Bonding with a significant adult is a key protective factor, especially for children living in poor or dangerous environments.

Part III
INTERNAL INTERVENTIONS STRATEGIES

II

BUILDING CONNECTIONS

Do more than exist . . . live.
Do more than touch . . . feel.
Do more than look . . . observe.
Do more than read . . . absorb.
Do more than hear . . . listen.
Do more than listen . . . understand.
Do more than think . . . ponder.
Do more than talk . . . say something.

—Thomas H. Rhoades

Setting up possibilities for children to build connections is an important undertaking. The benefits for a child who can build meaningful connections are indescribable. Connections should be built with significant adults, as well as with appropriate peers. Building connections also entails identification with larger groups. There are strategies for all of these.

STRATEGIES FOR BUILDING CONNECTIONS
WITH SIGNIFICANT ADULTS

1. Utilize Adopt-a-Student programs within your school. Organize teachers, social workers, counselors, librarians, aides, secretaries, janitors, playground supervisors, and anyone else that works at your building. Bring in parent volunteers. There are certain groups of children who specifically need to be targeted for such adoption. These groups include bullies, victims of bullying, and the transient/mobile population. These transient/mobile children are often part of the bullying problem either as the victim or as a bully. Any Adopt-a-Student program should at a minimum include checking on the adopted student on a regular basis, providing encouragement for them, and offering a safe place for them to come and talk or vent. Participating adults should establish a meaningful relationship with the adopted student.

2. Utilize Big Brother/Big Sister programs. Again, target specific students for these programs, including bullies, victims, and transient/mobile students. In fact, work with Big Brothers/Big Sisters programs to see if there are special grants or programs that can be used or developed for this purpose.

3. Call students by their first names. This is a good strategy to use with all students, but it is especially important for the bully, the victim, and transient/mobile students. Calling people by name creates a response in the brain that is important in both getting the brain's attention and building connections.

4. Accept students as they are, unconditionally. This does not mean you do not correct behavior, guide them into better choices, or expect improvement. It does mean that your acceptance of them as individuals is unconditional, not based on whether they follow every rule or get their homework in on time. Value the child.

5. Be creative in using tutors. Tutors have often been used to help students with math, but why not make it clear to tutors that a primary reason for the tutoring is to build connections.

6. Student transiency/mobility is a large and growing problem in our society. It can sneak up on a school without school officials realizing it until it is huge. I would recommend that any school look at its move-in/move-out statistics before automatically thinking this is not a problem. With mobile students it is important to have a system of getting them hooked up in ways to build connections immediately in order to slow the revolving door (Varlas, 2002). Don't wait for these students to start demonstrating problems. Patterns get set quickly, and if the wrong patterns get set it is that much more difficult to change. Another strategy for these students is to make sure you get them hooked up with connections outside of school. Hooking them up with a Big Brother/Big Sister can be crucial so that if they leave your school the connection can follow them.

7. A significant factor to keep in mind is not to wait for problems to develop. Develop a systematic approach that is ready and waiting, and target children for help. Those who need to be on the list for building connections include those students who move into your school during the year—the transient/mobile population. Also, target anyone who is a victim or a bully. Target children who are loners, or who are withdrawn or shy. Often children who could benefit most from building connections will be the very last to ask for help.

STRATEGIES FOR BUILDING CONNECTIONS BETWEEN STUDENTS

Building connections between students is a great way to cut down on bullying and victimization. When students get to know other students, it decreases the likelihood of bullying. Having a systematic way to accomplish this rather than leaving it to fate can significantly decrease the amount of bullying in any school. There are some simple yet effective ways of doing this.

1. Initiate a schoolwide effort to have students talk with each other the first 15 minutes of every day, or at least several times a week. This does not mean hanging out with friends, but meeting other students who are not with the group a student normally hangs out with. Although 15 minutes a day sounds like a lot of time to take away from instruction, the payoffs will be significant in many ways. Not only will bullying decrease, but if this is done first thing in the morning, high school and middle school students may be more awake when instruction actually begins so they will learn more efficiently.

2. Have assigned lunch tables for all students once a week. By doing so you can make sure students from different groups have the opportunity to interact.

3. Have specific times and events for students to meet others of different backgrounds. This could include a period of assigned tables for new students or for bullies and victims. The purpose of such assigned tables is not disciplinary but rather to provide opportunity to get to know others.

4. For writing assignments or social studies assignments, students can be assigned to interview other students who are different from themselves and write about the differences and the importance of having differences.

5. Use a "buddy system" approach for new students entering the building. This can be one buddy, but more preferable would be to have a group of buddies, each with the responsibility of showing the new student around for 1 day and introducing the new student to his or her friends.

6. Use students as Big Brothers/Big Sisters for younger or newer students. For example, have fifth- or sixth-grade students act as Big Brothers/Sisters for third- and fourth-grade

students. Have eighth-grade students act as Big Brothers/ Sisters for seventh-grade students. Have juniors and seniors act as Big Brothers/Sisters for freshmen and sophomores. Offer rewards, recognition, and praise for the students willing to act as Big Brothers/Big Sisters.

7. Get the student council involved in developing ways to make sure all students get connected. Have volunteers take other students to a ball game or a club, or invite them over for dinner. This, of course, takes parents to volunteer and participate, but the student council could take this on as a project.

OTHER STRATEGIES FOR BUILDING CONNECTIONS

Besides setting up specific ways for targeted students to build connections with adults or with other students, there are other strategies that can set up the opportunities for such connections to occur.

1. Encourage participation on sports teams. This can be a great opportunity to build a connection with the coach or coaches as well as with other team members.
2. Develop intramural sports opportunities.
3. Encourage participation in one or more of the other multiple school activities out there. This would include participation in school clubs, school intramurals, the school band or orchestra, the school choir, the drama club or school plays, the prom, school dances, or other school-sponsored events.
4. Honor or provide recognition to groups that gain new members.
5. Promote graduations and ceremonies. This includes graduation from third grade to fourth grade, from fifth to sixth, and so on. Invite parents to these events, and find special awards for every child (e.g., "The Most Improved in Math Award," "The Best Attitude Award," "The Best Act of Kindness Award,"

"The Best Big Brother Award"). While these may seem trivial to adults, this is recognition to a child who may be struggling. It may take a great deal of courage for some children to merely walk across a stage to receive a certificate. This builds connections to the class and to the school.

6. Promote acts of allegiance with students. This includes allegiance to our country. This can be done not merely by having different children lead the Pledge of Allegiance but also by having students talk about and write about what it means to be an American. This also includes allegiance to your state and to your school. What does it mean to be a Glenview Elementary School Eagle? How do we treat each other? How do we show we are proud of our school? This could include having pride days and cleanup days. Have certain students lead certain activities. This generates connections and bonding to your school.

7. Encourage participation in activities outside of school. This includes such things as Boy Scouts, Girl Scouts, Boys and Girls Clubs, summer camps, Little League, and activities sponsored for children through the library.

8. Take the time to find out and encourage what connections already exist for students, and use them to build other connections. Some students feel a connection to their families, some to a religion or church, some to a racial or ethnic group, some to a sports team, some to a certain identity. Accept children where they are, and encourage them to share with others who they are and what excites them. This bonds and connects.

CHAPTER SUMMARY/STRATEGIES

1. Building connections with significant adults, with peers, and with the larger group is important.

2. Utilize Adopt-a-Student programs.
3. Utilize Big Brothers/Big Sisters.
4. Call students by their first names.
5. Accept students as who they are unconditionally.
6. Use tutors creatively.
7. Target the transient/mobile students for help.
8. Target known bullies, known victims, and loners, or those students who appear withdrawn.
9. Initiate schoolwide efforts for students to get to know each other.
10. Have assigned lunch tables for all students once a week.
11. Have assigned lunch tables for targeted students.
12. Have students interview other students who are different from them.
13. Utilize a buddy system for new students.
14. Use students as Big Brothers/Big Sisters in a school effort.
15. Get the student council involved.
16. Encourage participation on sports teams.
17. Develop intramural sports opportunities.
18. Encourage participation in a wide range of school activities.
19. Honor school groups that gain new members.
20. Promote graduations and ceremonies.
21. Promote acts of allegiance to the larger group.
22. Encourage participation in activities outside of school.
23. Find out what connections and interests students already have and build on those.

12

BUILDING
EMOTIONAL INTELLIGENCE

I stood and watched the powerful Colorado River flow past.
Where did the river begin, I wondered? It began somewhere
as a single drop of water . . . joined by other drops. As a single
drop it has very little power; it cannot even flow by itself. As it
is joined by many other drops it flows, it becomes a force. Just
as we all need others. As I watched the Colorado I thought of
the many aspects of the river. First and foremost there was the
rapids, the white water. This is exciting, thrilling, fun, and
sometimes scary. The rapid moments pass quickly. Life can be
like that. After the rapids there came the eddies, little swirling
whirlpools that can suck you beneath the surface. Life can be
like that. There are the peaceful, slow stretches of the river
where life can flow gently and evenly and one can look back
and enjoy the scenery. Then there are the little coves where
one can pull in out of the current for a stop and a nap. In every
life there needs to be times of rest. The water was also very
cold, but on a hot day sometimes it felt good to get into the water, yet sometimes it felt better to get out. Change is important. I also noticed the wide canyon, the Grand Canyon. The
Colorado River didn't merely flow down this canyon; it made
this canyon. But it didn't make this canyon overnight. Some of

the most significant things we do in life are accomplished through little acts of patience and persistence . . . over time. As I watched the mighty Colorado I thought, all the important lessons in life are right here . . . flowing past, flowing away, flowing onward.

—Gary Plaford

BUILDING THE LANGUAGE OF EMOTIONAL INTELLIGENCE

It is important to build the emotional language of the child beyond *mad, glad, sad.*

1. Students need to be taught the "ABCs" of emotional language. Some students know only *mad, glad,* and *sad.* This is limiting in understanding and expressing their own feelings and in understanding and feeling empathy for others. Focus on teaching a broader range of words to express what they might feel. See "Appendix A: Emotional Vocabulary."
2. Utilize a matching test to determine emotional vocabulary so you know which students need to work on their emotional vocabulary and which already have this knowledge. See "Appendix B: Emotional Vocabulary Tests."
3. Have students select words from the emotional vocabulary and write about times they experienced these emotions.
4. When students read stories, have them select words from the emotional vocabulary (appendix A) and write about what emotions the characters demonstrated or might have felt.
5. Have students select words from the emotional vocabulary (appendix A) and act these words out for others to guess what they are feeling . . . like charades.
6. Have students role-play a scene of some kind. Assign each of them a specific emotion to portray in the scene, and have

the rest of the class guess what emotion each is acting out. The scene could be something related to getting bullied, or something like not getting selected for the team.

7. Select a word from the emotional vocabulary (appendix A). Ask the students to close their eyes and imagine what this specific emotion feels like. Then have the students visualize how to calm themselves or otherwise bring themselves back to a more peaceful, serene state. Use a different emotion every time, and then have the students discuss the most effective strategies for calming, relaxing, or returning to a positive state of mind.

8. Ask students to write about what emotions they see in the television shows or movies they watch. Discuss these in class.

9. Ask students to write about a situation where they were bullied or saw someone else bullied. Have them describe all the emotions they felt both during the bullying and afterward.

10. With all of these ideas, hold class discussions. Students can really learn about emotions from each other and from such discussions.

THE RELEVANCE OF EMOTIONS IN OUR LIVES

Besides building an emotional language, it is crucial to have discussions about the significance of emotions in our lives. How do emotions impact decisions? How do the decisions we make depend on emotions? What is the role of emotions in motivation?

1. Have classroom or small-group discussions about how the decisions we make are dependent on emotions. Have students discuss discipline issues, such as getting sent to the office, and how the emotions we have play a key role in the decisions that lead a student to get into trouble.

2. Have discussions about the careers students select and how emotions play a key role in how we choose careers and why people change jobs or careers.

3. Have discussions about how emotions influence our selection of boyfriends and girlfriends, and even eventually the person we marry.

4. Have discussions about what role emotions play in what students choose to do on a Friday or Saturday night. Don't we make decisions based on what we think will be fun, be exciting, or make us feel good?

5. Have students discuss how they would handle a situation where they need to get homework done, they want to talk with a friend on the telephone, and they want to go out later with some friends. What part do emotions play in their decisions in setting priorities?

6. Have a discussion on what role emotions play in motivation. What drives the student who becomes the star athlete, the student who becomes the best violinist, or the student who becomes the best at anything? Isn't it intense love of something, excitement, a sense of fulfillment, or fear that motivates us into action . . . or motivates us to become the best?

7. Have students role-play these same situations. The point is to make them aware, to help them realize that emotions play a key role in almost every decision they make.

CHAPTER SUMMARY/STRATEGIES

1. Teach students a broader emotional language.
2. Utilize emotional tests to learn which students need the most help with emotional language.
3. Have students select and write about emotions they have experienced.
4. Have students write about the emotions of characters they read about.

5. Use charades and games to act out emotions.
6. Have students role-play emotions.
7. Have students visualize emotions and emotional situations.
8. Have students write or talk about emotions they see on television.
9. Have students write or talk about emotions related to bullying.
10. Have classroom discussions about emotions.
11. Have discussions about how the decisions we make are dependent on emotions.
12. Have discussions about how emotions impact career decisions and career or job changes.
13. Have discussions about how emotions impact marriage decisions.
14. Have discussions about how emotions influence our choices about what we do for fun.
15. Have students discuss how emotions impact everyday decisions.
16. Have discussions about the role emotions play in motivation.
17. Have students role-play decision making as it relates to emotions.

⑬

EMOTIONAL TRIGGERS

No matter where we are in life there is always something changing. Change means losing comfortable old ways and replacing them with unfamiliar situations. Change goes hand in hand with fear. Sometimes the fear is so intense we would rather cling to something known regardless of how bad it is to avoid that fear. But change also goes hand in hand with growth. We cannot grow without change. We cannot grow without letting go. Change starts with endings. Change starts with letting go of the security of the old, looking fear in the eye for a period of time, and being willing to grow from the experience. Change, fear, and growth are all a part of the process. We cannot skip any part if we want to achieve the reward waiting at the end.

—Gary Plaford

RECOGNIZING EMOTIONAL TRIGGERS

Certain situations evoke certain responses in all of us. We all have these triggers. Take road rage, for example. Some people, even some very intelligent and educated people, become enraged by a driver who cuts them off. Most of these people will not pull out a gun to take care of the person who cut them off, but many will mutter profanities under their breath (or possibly not so much under their breath).

Another example comes when we visit home. Going back to see a parent, even for a mature adult, can stir old triggers very easily. Old responses, old feelings, or old habits that we had as teenagers can so quickly return.

Yet another example is that certain people set us off. Some people trigger a response in us that is always the same regardless of the setting or circumstance. These are the people we just want to—and try to—avoid.

In most of these situations, the resulting emotional triggers are not such significant things. For some, however, they are problematic.

MANAGING TRIGGERS IN STUDENTS

1. Learn what triggers certain students. Find out what sets them off. Some of this is merely through observation, but some can be through discussions with a student, with his parents, with past teachers, or sometimes with a school social worker or counselor. Typically when looking at triggers, we focus on what triggers students to anger and to strike out at others. That is certainly important. It is also important, however, to recognize triggers that evoke internal strife and self-destruction, as well as triggers that evoke depression.

2. Observe behavior. When a student loses control and acts out, don't merely deal with the behavior. Go back and find out what led up to it. Ask what others saw or did. When the student regains control, talk to her to find out from her perspective what happened—what led up to the point of her losing control. Chart this behavior. This can be valuable in understanding what sets someone off.

3. In looking at what sets a student off, look for habitual thought patterns. Does he have specific thought habits? For example, does the student always say/think, "I can't do it," when looking at a new task? Does she always say/think, "I'm not good enough?" Does he always say/think, "Nobody likes me?" These and other habitual ways of thinking can trigger a negative response to events that lead to losing control. If you can recognize what the habitual thoughts are, which are the triggers of negative responses and behaviors, then you can challenge those thoughts and change behaviors.

4. It is also important to understand types of situations that trigger a loss of control for a student. For example, some students desperately need structure and routine. Without structure and routine, they fall apart. If you know that, it becomes important to plan ahead as much as possible to make sure these students are not placed in situations where there is little or no structure. It is important to always have some routines worked out for those students.

5. When you see a situation or habitual negative thought pattern beginning, it is important to step in and divert the behavior to something else, or at least provide the student with an opportunity for a time-out on her own. Recognizing the structural and internal triggers for negative behaviors allows you to step in and reroute events before they reach the point of no return.

SELF-MONITORING TRIGGERS

1. Once you recognize structural situations and habitual thought patterns that trigger anger, rage, loss of control, lashing out, self-destruction, or depression in a student, it is possible to help the student learn to recognize those same things. That is the ultimate goal. As a teacher you can intervene in school to divert such outbreaks, but the student will

not always be a student—he needs to be able to recognize his triggers and intervene on his own.

2. Help the student recognize what structural events, events in the outside world that she has no control over, set her off or trigger negative responses.

3. Once the student recognizes such events, help him devise his own strategies for either removing himself from such situations or putting structure and routine in his personal environment so he can cope with the triggering event more successfully.

4. Help the student recognize patterns of habitual thought she may have that trigger negative emotional responses and negative behaviors.

5. Help the student alter his negative thoughts by replacing them with more positive thought habits. For the student who habitually thinks, "I can't do this," help him replace that thought with "This is a new situation. I don't know yet if I can do it or not, but I will never know unless I try. I am brave enough to try." This will not always be successful, but the point is the student will start to learn that behaviors stem from thoughts, and through controlling our thoughts we can control our behaviors.

6. For the student who has notable triggers, try to instill the habit of using language as a strategy (i.e., tell the story of what happened or is happening). Stories are powerful because they move some of the locus of control out of the limbic system, the emotional center, and into the language center. Putting thoughts into words has a calming effect, thereby helping the student avoid some negative actions.

CHAPTER SUMMARY/STRATEGIES

1. There are events that trigger emotional responses in all of us.

2. Road rage or being caught up in past emotions and behaviors when visiting parents are examples of the effect of such triggers.
3. Learning what triggers emotions such as rage, as well as self-destructive emotions, is valuable.
4. Don't merely respond to behaviors. Be a detective in finding out what set the behaviors off.
5. Habitual thought patterns can also be emotional triggers.
6. Lack of or loss of structure and routine can trigger emotional episodes.
7. Recognizing triggers allows you to step in and reroute the situation to safer ground.
8. The ultimate goal is to help students recognize and deal with their own triggers.
9. Help students recognize outside events that trigger their emotional responses.
10. Help students devise strategies for coping with or removing themselves from such events.
11. Help students recognize habitual thought patterns that trigger negative emotional responses.
12. Help students develop alternative, more positive thought habits.
13. Help students learn the value of language and putting events and emotions into stories as a way of both calming and coping.

14

CREATING AN OUTWARD FOCUS

Imagine a bank that credits your account each and every morning with $86,400. It carries over no balance from day to day. Every evening it deletes whatever part of the balance you failed to use during the day. What would you do? Would you let the balance be taken from you every day, or would you make every effort to draw it out? Each of us has such a bank. It is called TIME. Every morning it credits you with 86,400 seconds. Every evening it writes off, as lost, every second you have failed to use to good purpose. It allows no overdraft. Each day it opens a new account for you. Each night it burns the remains of the day. If you fail to use the day's deposits, the loss is yours. There is no going back. There is no drawing against tomorrow. You must live in the present on today's deposits. Invest it so as to get from it the utmost in health, happiness, and success. The clock is running. Make the most of today, for today is the one and only day you will be able to do so.

—Unknown

One key in building empathy and building connections is to focus outside oneself. Focus on serving others. This also teaches the individual who is serving others more about himself or herself. It helps that individual learn what is important and what he or she enjoys. You don't learn that from looking inward, from introspection, from belly button gazing. You learn that from focusing outside yourself. What makes you special in this world is what you do, not what you think about. In *Man's Search for Meaning*, Victor Frankl (1963) uses the analogy of youth's fascination with the boomerang. The young person thinks the boomerang is a wonderful toy because you throw it and it comes back to you. But that is wrong, says Frankl. Ask any Aborigine. The boomerang is a weapon used for hunting. The one that comes back to you is the one that has missed the mark. So when it comes back, you must pick it up and throw it again. What is important is what you are aiming for out there.

What is important for our children is to provide opportunities for service to others. This not only builds empathy for others and builds connections and the opportunity for connections with others but also helps children learn who they are and what is important in their lives.

PROVIDING OPPORTUNITIES FOR SERVICE TO OTHERS

1. Provide opportunities for young children to help in the classroom. Let students feed the class pet, clean the chalkboards, run errands. And don't forget to provide recognition for the help they give.
2. Provide opportunities to help around school: help the janitor, help plant a tree, help clean up the playground, and so on.
3. Have students serve as Project Peace monitors, or in other such positions where they can act as mediators in conflicts between other students. This involves selection and training of these students, but a great deal is gained from these experiences.
4. Allow students to tutor younger students in math or reading.

5. Provide opportunities for students to write letters to residents of nursing homes, or children in children's hospitals, or children less fortunate who live in other countries.

6. Encourage participation in the March of Dimes or other fund-raising events. Take the time to discuss what these events are for and whom they help.

7. Initiate or provide opportunities for service learning projects.

8. Take field trips to social service agencies to learn what they are doing and whom they help.

9. Take working field trips to social service agencies where the students get a chance to do some of the work needed.

10. Visit Habitat for Humanity to see how others volunteer to build homes for those who could otherwise never afford one.

11. Set up and encourage volunteering in nursing homes, senior citizen homes, hospitals, social service agencies, animal shelters, and the like.

12. Give awards for individuals as well as for the class when students find ways to be of service to others.

13. Discuss the importance of serving others with parents, and encourage them to find ways for their children to do this.

14. Have discussions with the class about unique ways they can think of to be of help to others. Provide recognition for the most creative ways students come up with to help others.

15. Have discussions with the class about the importance of these activities, not just for the people you help but also for what it does for you when you help.

CHAPTER SUMMARY/STRATEGIES

1. Building empathy and building connections both require an outward focus.

2. Service to others is a valuable tool in creating such an out-ward focus.
3. Provide opportunities for students to help in the classroom.
4. Provide opportunities for students to help around school.
5. Have students serve as conflict mediators at school.
6. Allow older students to tutor younger students.
7. Provide opportunities for students to write letters to nursing home residents.
8. Encourage participation in fund-raising events such as the March of Dimes.
9. Encourage service learning opportunities.
10. Take field trips to social service agencies.
11. Take working field trips to such agencies.
12. Visit Habitat for Humanity sites to see hands-on examples of people helping other people.
13. Encourage volunteering in nursing homes, hospitals, and so on.
14. Provide recognition and awards for service to others.
15. Encourage parents to promote service to others to their children.
16. Have class discussions about unique ways students can think of to help others.
17. Have classroom discussions about what serving others does for others, and what it does for the one helping.

15

THE MAGIC OF ROUTINE

Boundaries, limits, and expectations are thought of by some people in our society as negative. It's like telling a child "No," it limits the child. In reality, setting boundaries and limits is not negative at all. Far from it. A boat taken out of the water is not really free to be a boat. Only in the confines of the water is it free to explore its limits and potential. Only in the water can it choose its own direction and speed. Likewise, only when we give children boundaries and structure are they really free to safely and fully explore their potential.

—Unknown

Structure and routine can be accomplished on several levels. It can be built into the student's day, it can be established in how the student responds to situations and events, and it can be incorporated into how a student thinks.

DAILY STRUCTURE

1. Talk with students so they know what to expect. This means not only talking with students before special events but also talking with them at the end of each day about what to expect for tomorrow. It also means talking through what you expect of them during events or during the day.

2. Post a schedule for the day. Sometimes you might even post a schedule for a specific lesson. For example, a lesson might include the following:
   a. Teacher-led instruction
   b. Small-group discussion
   c. Writing assignment

3. Some students need more structure and routine than others. Make the effort to find out which students do require more structure, and make building structure into their day the first priority.

4. Students who are repeat victims of bullies should be high on the list for having structure built into their day. Talk through exactly what the victim's day will look like. For example, sit down with the victim and discuss what door he will enter, what hallway he will come down, that he will stop by the counselor's office on the way to his locker to check in, what hallway he will take to his first-period class, what hallway he will take to the next period, that on the way he will stop to check in with Mr. Smith, that he will check in with the counselor on the way to his next class, and so on. Giving students a structure for the day settles them. It is calming. And if something out of the ordinary happens (e.g., someone threatens them), it puts that into a perspective rather than immediately sending them into fight-or-flight mode. For some students, talking through their schedule provides enough structure to help them get through the day. As stated earlier in this book, the first two conditions that create stress are

novelty and unpredictability. By talking through a student's day in specific detail, you can lessen some of the novelty and unpredictability, thus decreasing the student's stress level.

5. Building structure into the day for a bully is also important. Such structure can fill her day so that she does not have the downtime to plan or think about bullying another.

RESPONSE ROUTINE

1. Structure can also be utilized in building routine into the way a student responds to situations. Teaching the student how to problem solve is important. In other words, teach him what steps he needs to take in responding to situations or events when those types of situations arise or events occur. This should not be left to chance. An automatic set of steps (i.e., habitual responses) empowers him to act decisively, and it calms him to have such a practiced strategy in mind. Those mental steps could include the following:
   a. What are all the responses I could make?
   b. What outcome do I really want?
   c. Which of these responses will most likely get me that outcome?
   d. Now, what should I do?
2. Likewise, when a victim is specifically confronted with bullying, the plan for the victim could be as follows:
   a. Tell the bully, "Stop it!"
   b. Get away from the scene.
   c. Tell someone in authority.
3. Another important response to teach victims is how to calm or relax themselves. Giving them such techniques puts them in control of managing their responses, which is the ultimate goal. This can be taught in a variety of ways. Deep breathing, meditation, yoga, tai chi, and biofeedback all elicit a calming

response. All these techniques move the locus of control out
of the limbic system, where fight or flight can be triggered,
and into the left hemisphere of the brain, where routine is
monitored.

4. Have discussions with students to help them understand the
   importance and the calming effect of routine. It helps if they
   understand the basics of altering the part of their brain in control at a given moment and how they can do this for themselves.

THOUGHT STRUCTURE

1. As mentioned before, having a student talk through her day
   is important. This puts the plan for the day into language.
   Putting it into language moves it out of the limbic system so
   it can be discussed more rationally rather than merely being
   a fear or dread of something unspecific.

2. Building routine into thought structure is of great importance. As mentioned earlier, some students have negative
   thought patterns or habits (Amen, 1999). In fact all students
   have these; all people have these. It is just that some are
   much more negative and destructive than others. Listen for
   these in students, and when the negative and unproductive
   ones are heard, target those to challenge and change.

3. Also mentioned earlier was the strategy of setting expectations for students. This can be taken a step further. Expectations can also be set for the evening when they are at
   home. Teachers often assign homework, and the expectation is that students will do it. Some will, but the expectation is not clearly stated. Even saying, "Do your homework,"
   is not stating an expectation clearly enough for some students. By stating something like "John, I expect you to do
   your homework tonight," you are making a connection between you, the teacher, and John, the student, that you expect the homework to be done. This expectation can and

certainly should be stated to the class as a whole, but it should be stated specifically to certain students who have trouble getting their work done. Use the name of those students in speaking directly to them, but do this privately, not in front of the class. That will tend to have the opposite effect. This practice establishes clear expectations between you and John. Patience is also key here. Doing this once or even a few times may not have much impact, but repeatedly done it will start to create habits of thought in John. Eventually during the evening, John will start having the thought, "The teacher expects me to do my homework." The thoughts have to be there before the behaviors will follow, and we can develop neural pathways for the kind of thinking we want in students.

4. If, in a bully or victim, you see thought routines or habits that lead to bullying or victimization, those thought habits can be challenged and replaced with alternative thoughts. This was discussed with emotional triggers. A student who habitually and automatically says, "I can't do it," is demonstrating a lack of confidence and self-esteem. This can easily result in that student becoming a likely target of bullying. Hence, targeting that sort of routine thinking can deter victimization. Likewise, some bullies demonstrate through their habitual thoughts and actions that they crave being the center of attention, and by bullying they achieve that. By finding a more positive manner in which they can achieve the attention they crave, and establishing and nurturing that thought in them, you can often supplant bullying behaviors. The point is to see what thought routines exist and know that if negative or destructive thought patterns and habits exist, they can be supplanted by creating more productive ones.

5. After an incident of bullying, ask the bully what he was thinking. Every time he is caught bullying, ask him this question. Eventually both you and he will start to recognize patterns of thought that can be challenged.

ROUTINE AND STRESS

1. The four conditions of stress are novelty, unpredictability, low sense of control, and threat to ego. Finding ways to address each of these through routine is valuable.
2. Talk through new situations, and use techniques such as visualization or role-play to take the novelty out of potentially new and stressful events.
3. Discuss situations with students specifically aimed at helping them predict outcomes. This goes hand in hand with teaching problem solving.
4. All the strategies we can give students that empower them to deal with a situation or with their response to a situation will give them control.
5. Mastery involves finding what you love through play, practicing what you love, and then getting better at it day by day. Some children do not understand that they are mastering skills even though they are. Helping students learn what mastery is and helping them recognize it in themselves helps them gain confidence and esteem and counters some of the threat many students feel regarding their ego.

CHAPTER SUMMARY/STRATEGIES

1. Structure and routine can be built into the day, into how the student responds to events, and into how the student thinks about events.
2. We can build structure by talking with students about the structure of the day and what they should expect.
3. We can post a schedule for each day.
4. We can learn which students require the most structure and routine and make the effort to accommodate those higher needs.

5. Repeat victims of bullying should be high on the list for providing extra structure and routine.
6. Building structure for the known bully is also effective.
7. Teaching students how to problem solve empowers them to act decisively and calmly rather than merely react as usual.
8. The victim of bullying can be taught a specific strategy, such as the following:
   a. Say, "Stop that!"
   b. Get away from the scene.
   c. Tell someone.
9. Teach victims how to calm or relax themselves.
10. Have classroom discussions about the importance and value of calming routines.
11. Teaching students how to talk through their day, how to put it into language, is calming.
12. Listen for and challenge negative and destructive thought habits.
13. Set and communicate specific expectations for specific students.
14. Listen especially for habitual thought patterns in bullies and victims, and challenge those.
15. Ask the bully what she was thinking—every time she bullies— to learn her thought habits.
16. Utilize routine to specifically address the four conditions of stress: novelty, unpredictability, low sense of control, and threat to ego.

FINAL THOUGHTS

There was once a cliff on the edge of the town, and there was a beautiful park at the top of the cliff. The children of the town would play in the park, and sometimes they would fall off the cliff. Children would often be hurt, some quite badly. The town elders cared about the children and put an ambulance at the bottom of the cliff to take the unfortunate victims to the hospital. In fact, the town finally kept an ambulance at the bottom of the cliff all the time for the sake of its children.

One day a concerned citizen asked, "Wouldn't it be better to build a fence at the top of the cliff and keep the children from falling?"

"Why should we build a fence at the top when we have such a nice ambulance at the bottom?" asked the elders. And so they continued to carry the injured children to the hospital in the fine ambulance, and shook their heads at the tragedy of it all.

—Unknown

Bullying happens in our society, and it happens in societies around the world. Bullying is not a new phenomenon; it has gone on since the beginning of time. Some bullying has the purpose of establishing the pecking order in a society. Some bullying is the result of competition. Some bullying occurs because of the need to enforce social norms and conformity to those norms. At some times in some societies, enforcing norms and establishing a pecking order were necessary for the survival of the group. However, we do not live in tribal communities any longer, and the survival of the clan does not depend on the precise conformity of each member. The larger norms are certainly enforced by the laws of the land, but in this day and age we can afford to have people in society who are different.

In fact, differences are what give life novelty and hence make life exciting. It is true that novelty can cause stress, but stress and excitement often go hand in hand. Why do people jump out of airplanes, ride roller coasters, visit places they have never seen? The brain seeks novelty. The brain seeks to learn. Sometimes educators will say their students aren't paying attention. But the brain is always paying attention—it just may not be to what the teacher wants. The key is to focus that attention. Utilizing novelty can help us do that.

It is the newness in life, the novelty, the differences that we encounter that cause the brain to create new neural pathways. This keeps the brain engaged; this keeps the brain learning. The brain will continue to learn as long as we continue to feed it new and exciting information. That is what keeps us young. That is what will help ward off such conditions as Alzheimer's. Elderly people who read and engage in active dialogue and debate have a far greater chance of avoiding Alzheimer's than do elderly people who sit in front of a television all day. It is difference, it is novelty, it is change that does this for the brain and hence for the individual.

Think about how bored you would be if you ate the same meal every day, if you had a job where you tightened the same nut on the same bolt on the same assembly line every day, if you sat and watched the exact same movie every evening. It is difference that makes life exciting, that makes life worth living. Yet we fear change and mistrust difference. Isn't that ironic.

For many children, school is often the first place they meet people different from themselves. Furthermore, school is often the first place children experience bullying. Coincidence? If parents have not taught children to expect and value difference and diversity in others at an early age, the school experience may be a shock. Where parents have taught children to devalue and mistrust difference and diversity, there will be intolerance and friction. If we believe that people who are different from us in some ways are different in every way, we are wrong. The similarities we have with others far outweigh the differences. But it is the differences that make each of us unique and exciting. Focusing on these differences as all encompassing rather than as the subtle nuances that keep the world interesting is often the basis for bullying.

Bullying is harmful. It creates stress, for the victim and often for the bystanders. Yet some adults have the misconception that being bullied is good for children, that it toughens them up, that it builds character. When we are on the job at our place of work, do we really think that being bullied or harassed will make us tougher . . . will build our character? School is a child's place of work. Why would anyone think that being bullied is good for a child? The theory that whatever doesn't kill you makes you a better person doesn't apply here. In fact, continued victimization is so stressful that even if the victim does not commit suicide (which is the third leading cause of death in teenagers in the United States), it impacts the hippocampus and makes the brain unable to effectively manage stress for the rest of the individual's life. That is not toughening kids up. Far from it.

Another misconception many adults have, including both parents and educators, is that there really isn't much bullying at *our* school. This misconception exists because adults don't see a lot of it and because adults don't hear much about it. Adults don't see it because children are not stupid. Most children will not get caught in the act of bullying. Most children, if and when they bully another, will do it at the bus stop, on the playground, in the restroom, in the lunchroom, or at least when the teacher's back is turned. It's only when the teacher turns unexpectedly that the student ever gets caught.

Adults don't hear much about bullying because children won't tell adults. There are several reasons for this. First, there is the code of silence. "It is bad to be a snitch" is the general thinking. Adults who tell children not to be a tattletale reinforce that code. Another reason children won't talk about bullying is that they are afraid the bully will hurt them even more if the bully finds out they told. After all, the bully will often say, "If you tell, I'll really get you!"

Another factor is the belief children have that nothing can be done. The fact that bullying exists at the level it does is a clear indication to children that adults cannot stop it. Or it is an indication that adults don't care, which is the final reason children don't tell. Adults believe that if bullying was really bad our children would tell us, and children are thinking there is no way they will tell adults. Thus, both groups live with their own little misperceptions—and bullying thrives.

A misconception that parents often have is that we know our child and he or she would not be a party to bullying. The truth is our judgment of our children is clouded. We develop a perception of who our children are and what they are like, and it is difficult to see them in a different light. Let's think through this for a moment. How many roles do you play in your life? Are you a parent, a spouse, a lover, a friend, a son or daughter, an employee, a boss, a manager, a coworker, a consumer, a fan? The roles we play do impact our behavior. Children also play many different roles, and they are also experimenting with who they are, developing an identity. As parents we do not often see all the roles our children play. To be effective as parents, we cannot always assume the best of our children. We can hope for the best, but we must accept that they will make mistakes. To believe that our children are incapable of such behavior as bullying is to parent with our eyes closed, and that does an injustice to our children because it keeps us from providing proper correction and direction. Being a parent involves lots of wonderful, loving moments, but it also involves some tough times holding our children accountable.

Another misconception is that things are just the way they are, things have always been this way, it was good enough before, so why rock the boat? Systems are hard to change. Systems have a life of their own. That does not mean they cannot change or they should not change. Our world is changing every day. Technology certainly forces change at a very rapid rate, but technology has also allowed us to learn a great deal and has given us the opportunity to change. What we have learned about the brain and how it functions certainly gives us the opportunity—and, I believe, the mandate—to use that information to deal with such issues as bullying. We can make a difference through both the external and the internal interventions we have discussed. We can make the learning process so much better and healthier for children.

There is one analogy that states that if you stick your hand in a bucket of water, then pull it out, the hole that is left is the amount you will be missed when you are gone. I believe that is wrong. There is another analogy that I believe is more accurate. A father and son watched a ship as it loaded up at the dock and set sail. They watched the beautiful white sails of the ship far into the distance until it could no longer be seen. "It is gone," said the son. "No, it is not gone," corrected the father. "It is still there. We can no longer see it, but the ship still exists. As long as you can picture that ship in your mind, it will continue to exist for you."

What we do for our children, for our students, will always exist. The treasures of kindness, acceptance, understanding, and love will forevermore be with them and, I am sure, will continue to be passed along by those who have received them.

APPENDIX A:
EMOTIONAL VOCABULARY

afraid
alone
amused
annoyed
attractive
awesome
awful
belittled
bitter
bored
bummed out
calm
cautious
concerned
confused
content
crabby
defeated
disappointed

discouraged
dumb
eager
elated
encouraged
enraged
enthusiastic
excited
explosive
fearful
frustrated
funky
funny
furious
glad
goofy
great
gullible
hollow

hopeful
hopeless
hurt
inadequate
interested
irritated
jealous
joyful
lonesome
lost
lovable
mad
messed up
mindless
miserable
mushy
needed
nervous
open
optimistic
overwhelmed
paranoid
pent up
powerful
powerless

pushed
rageful
rejected
resentful
respected
sad
safe
scared
shallow
shamed
silly
stupid
surprised
tense
terrible
threatened
together
tolerant
unimportant
unloved
unsure
valued
victimized
wanted
worried

APPENDIX B:
EMOTIONAL VOCABULARY TESTS

EMOTIONAL VOCABULARY TEST #1

a. content
b. jealous
c. afraid
d. powerful
e. hurt
f. awful
g. silly
h. victimized

i. belittled
j. funny
k. lost

l. unloved

m. sad
n. discouraged

___ filled with fear
___ treated as small or unimportant
___ satisfied, happy
___ lacking hope or spirit
___ tight, taut, nervous
___ easily deceived or duped
___ engulfed or submerged in turmoil
___ envious, apprehensive, bitter over lost affection
___ harmed or injured by another
___ capable, forceful, dynamic, strong
___ lacking affection, warmth, acceptance from others
___ helpless, bewildered, unable to find one's way
___ annoyed, impatient, inflamed
___ bad, unpleasant, terrible

o. tense   ___ inspired, filled with hope or
                            confidence
p. concerned   ___ explosive, angry, furious
q. rageful   ___ feeling pain, distress, suffering
r. encouraged   ___ sorrowful, unhappy, gloomy
s. overwhelmed   ___ amusing or odd
t. gullible   ___ interested, anxious, troubled
u. irritated   ___ lacking good sense, foolish

EMOTIONAL VOCABULARY TEST #1 SCORING KEY

a. content   _c_ filled with fear
b. jealous   _i_ treated as small or unimportant
c. afraid   _a_ satisfied, happy
d. powerful   _n_ lacking hope or spirit
e. hurt   _o_ tight, taut, nervous
f. awful   _t_ easily deceived or duped
g. silly   _s_ engulfed or submerged in turmoil
h. victimized   _b_ envious, apprehensive, bitter over
                        lost affection
i. belittled   _h_ harmed or injured by another
j. funny   _d_ capable, forceful, dynamic, strong
k. lost   _l_ lacking affection, warmth,
                        acceptance from others
l. unloved   _k_ helpless, bewildered, unable to find
                        one's way
m. sad   _u_ annoyed, impatient, inflamed
n. discouraged   _f_ bad, unpleasant, terrible
o. tense   _r_ inspired, filled with hope or
                        confidence
p. concerned   _q_ explosive, angry, furious
q. rageful   _e_ feeling pain, distress, suffering
r. encouraged   _m_ sorrowful, unhappy, gloomy
s. overwhelmed   _j_ amusing or odd

t. gullible   _p_ interested, anxious, troubled
u. irritated   _g_ lacking good sense, foolish

EMOTIONAL VOCABULARY TEST #2

a. scared   ___ explosive, angry, furious
b. terrible   ___ incapable, insufficient
c. alone   ___ careless, heedless, lacking sense
d. awesome   ___ unaccepted, not included, outcast
e. crabby   ___ doubtful, uncertain
f. glad   ___ apart, solitary, separate
g. rejected   ___ dissatisfied, unfulfilled
h. unsure   ___ alluring, charming, charismatic
i. wanted   ___ accessible, candid, accepting
j. eager   ___ superb, outstanding, inspiring
k. open   ___ disgraced, dishonored, embarrassed
l. enraged   ___ frightened, panicked, afraid
m. inadequate   ___ joyful, pleasant, happy
n. funky   ___ expectant, waiting, interested
o. mad   ___ ill-tempered, quarrelsome
p. pent up   ___ desired, accepted, belonging to
q. attractive   ___ dreadful, bad, severe
r. disappointed   ___ confined, constricted, tied up
s. hollow   ___ unusual, blue, down, depressed
t. shamed   ___ unhappy, irritated
u. mindless   ___ empty, devoid of

EMOTIONAL VOCABULARY TEST #2 SCORING KEY

a. scared   _l_ explosive, angry, furious
b. terrible   _m_ incapable, insufficient
c. alone   _u_ careless, heedless, lacking sense
d. awesome   _g_ unaccepted, not included, outcast

e. crabby	_h_	doubtful, uncertain
f. glad	_c_	apart, solitary, separate
g. rejected	_r_	dissatisfied, unfulfilled
h. unsure	_q_	alluring, charming, charismatic
i. wanted	_k_	accessible, candid, accepting
j. eager	_d_	superb, outstanding, inspiring
k. open	_t_	disgraced, dishonored, embarrassed
l. enraged	_a_	frightened, panicked, afraid
m. inadequate	_f_	joyful, pleasant, happy
n. funky	_j_	expectant, waiting, interested
o. mad	_e_	ill-tempered, quarrelsome
p. pent up	_i_	desired, accepted, belonging to
q. attractive	_b_	dreadful, bad, severe
r. disappointed	_p_	confined, constricted, tied up
s. hollow	_n_	unusual, blue, down, depressed
t. shamed	_o_	unhappy, irritated
u. mindless	_s_	empty, devoid of

EMOTIONAL VOCABULARY TEST #3

a. bitter	___	beaten, thwarted, unsuccessful
b. annoyed	___	composed, undisturbed
c. elated	___	secure, protected
d. defeated	___	troubled, uneasy, anxious
e. frustrated	___	sentimental, emotional, romantic
f. lonesome	___	hopeful, expecting the best
g. mushy	___	menaced, in danger, in peril
h. safe	___	disappointed, spiteful, malevolent, unpalatable
i. shallow	___	uninterested, unexcited, dull
j. threatened	___	angry, raging
k. worried	___	curious, concerned, focused
l. furious	___	filled with joy, delighted
m. needed	___	feeling secluded, alone, desolate

n. interested   ___ feeling offended, indignant, wronged

o. unimportant   ___ trivial, superficial, not profound

p. pushed   ___ defeated, thwarted, baffled

q. bored   ___ disturbed, bothered, vexed, irritated

r. resentful   ___ interested, inspired, impassioned

s. calm   ___ insignificant, common, unessential

t. optimistic   ___ desired, wanted, appreciated, required

u. excited   ___ pressured, forced, coerced, shoved

EMOTIONAL VOCABULARY TEST #3 SCORING KEY

a. bitter   _d_ beaten, thwarted, unsuccessful

b. annoyed   _s_ composed, undisturbed

c. elated   _h_ secure, protected

d. defeated   _k_ troubled, uneasy, anxious

e. frustrated   _g_ sentimental, emotional, romantic

f. lonesome   _t_ hopeful, expecting the best

g. mushy   _j_ menaced, in danger, in peril

h. safe   _a_ disappointed, spiteful, malevolent, unpalatable

i. shallow   _q_ uninterested, unexcited, dull

j. threatened   _l_ angry, raging

k. worried   _n_ curious, concerned, focused

l. furious   _c_ filled with joy, delighted

m. needed   _f_ feeling secluded, alone, desolate

n. interested   _r_ feeling offended, indignant, wronged

o. unimportant   _i_ trivial, superficial, not profound

p. pushed   _e_ defeated, thwarted, baffled

q. bored   _b_ disturbed, bothered, vexed, irritated

r. resentful   _u_ interested, inspired, impassioned

s. calm   _o_ insignificant, common, unessential

t. optimistic   __m__ desired, wanted, appreciated,
                                   required
u. excited   __p__ pressured, forced, coerced, shoved

EMOTIONAL VOCABULARY TEST # 4

a. joyful   ____ perplexed, bewildered
b. cautious   ____ apprehensive, panic-stricken,
                                   frightened
c. amused   ____ encouraged, reassured, optimistic
d. great   ____ jumpy, jittery, uneasy, tense
e. hopeful   ____ weak, incapable, unable, ineffective
f. surprised   ____ dull, ignorant, slow-witted
g. enthusiastic   ____ precious, worthy, estimable
h. explosive   ____ pleased, tickled, entertained
i. fearful   ____ excited, interested, passionate
j. hopeless   ____ wary, vigilant, careful
k. goofy   ____ admired, revered, looked up to
l. paranoid   ____ open, respectful of differences,
                                   accepting
m. stupid   ____ in harmony, coordinated, organized
n. lovable   ____ angry, furious, potentially violent
o. confused   ____ despairing, dejected, pessimistic
p. nervous   ____ astounded, startled, caught off guard
q. valued   ____ persecuted, watched, suspected
r. tolerant   ____ elated, happy, ecstatic
s. powerless   ____ silly, careless, frivolous, lacking
                                   judgment
t. together   ____ distinguished, remarkable, larger
                                   than life
u. respected   ____ charming, adorable, engaging,
                                   beloved

EMOTIONAL VOCABULARY TEST #4 SCORING KEY

a. joyful

b. cautious

c. amused

d. great

e. hopeful

f. surprised

g. enthusiastic

h. explosive

i. fearful

j. hopeless

k. goofy

l. paranoid

m. stupid

n. lovable

o. confused

p. nervous

q. valued

r. tolerant

s. powerless

t. together

u. respected

__o__ perplexed, bewildered

__i__ apprehensive, panic-stricken, frightened

__e__ encouraged, reassured, optimistic

__p__ jumpy, jittery, uneasy, tense

__s__ weak, incapable, unable, ineffective

__m__ dull, ignorant, slow-witted

__q__ precious, worthy, estimable

__c__ pleased, tickled, entertained

__g__ excited, interested, passionate

__b__ wary, vigilant, careful

__u__ admired, revered, looked up to

__r__ open, respectful of differences, accepting

__t__ in harmony, coordinated, organized

__h__ angry, furious, potentially violent

__j__ despairing, dejected, pessimistic

__f__ astounded, startled, caught off guard

__l__ persecuted, watched, suspected

__a__ elated, happy, ecstatic

__k__ silly, careless, frivolous, lacking judgment

__d__ distinguished, remarkable, larger than life

__n__ charming, adorable, engaging, beloved

APPENDIX C:
STUDY AND PLANNING GUIDE

This study guide is divided into two parts. The first part is a chapter-by-chapter look at the issues discussed in *Bullying and the Brain*. The questions posed in this section will hopefully make you think about your school and the children you encounter. They will also guide some thought toward ways you might manage some of the issues, promoting a deeper understanding, knowledge, and appreciation for some of the things in our lives that we tend to take for granted.

The second part of this guide is a plan of action. It takes the major themes and strategies presented in *Bullying and the Brain* and asks that you think about what strategies or aspects of the strategies could be applied in your school . . . in your classroom . . . with your kids . . . with the children you work with. This is in no way a prepackaged program. Often prepackaged programs are not successful, and there are several reasons for this. The first is that prepackaged programs treat every school as if it were the same as all other schools. Schools are different—very different. To make every school fit into the same mold, like forcing square pegs into round holes, is not feasible; further, it does not validate the differences or the worth of the school.

Second, for any effort addressing bullying to be successful, the staff at the school must buy into it . . . be a part of it. They need ownership of it. A prepackaged program does not create or promote that ownership. Individual and staff discussions and planning regarding which strategies could and should be implemented at a specific school, and how to do so, provide that very necessary buy-in, that ownership, that accountability. Finally, prepackaged programs are always an add-on to the work teachers already do. Most teachers work very hard at their jobs, and the time spent during the school day is planned down to the minute. Add-on programs simply won't get done—no matter how good a program might be—because teachers don't have enough time in the day to add something else on. Many of the strategies in this book can be interwoven into the regular day, into regular subjects, into regular activities. As discussions are held, it will become easier to see how this is possible. Along with gaining the knowledge of why something is valuable and how it works, we can embed our understanding into ongoing strategies to counter bullying. What is important is that the strategies become part of the culture of the school . . . a "this is how we do it here" mentality.

Having said that, I wish you the very best of luck in your efforts to address this very important and very timely issue with and for our youth. Our youth are our future. They deserve the best. They certainly deserve our best.

INTRODUCTION

1. What is the culture at your school? Is it one that is conducive to bullying or not conducive to bullying? How can you tell? What indications are there to support your thinking?
2. How much bullying really goes on at your school? How prevalent is it? Do you know this as fact, or are you making assumptions based mainly on what you don't know?
3. Is there agreement from everyone involved regarding how much bullying goes on? Does the faculty, do the parents, and

do the students all agree about this? Do you really know what parents think about bullying issues at your school? Do you really know what other faculty and staff think about this issue? Have students been asked for their input?

4. Would a survey on bullying and school safety be productive or necessary? If it is necessary, why is it necessary? Is it to find out if bullying exists? Is it to find out the level at which it exists? Or is it to prove to certain factions that it exists?

CHAPTER 1: WHAT PARENTS AND THE COMMUNITY MUST KNOW

1. Do the parents of children at your school agree about the definition of what bullying is and what it encompasses?
2. Are parents aware that bullying goes on at your school? How do you know this? What has been done to share that information?
3. How can we effectively communicate with parents so that information can be shared both ways and so that consensus can be reached and plans implemented?
4. How can parents be effectively utilized in managing the bullying issue at your school? What is the number one job you would ask parents to do?

CHAPTER 2: WHAT EDUCATORS MUST KNOW

1. Does the faculty at your school agree on the definition of bullying?
2. Is the faculty in agreement that bullying does happen at your school? How do you know? Has this been discussed?
3. If the faculty agrees that bullying does occur at your school, does the faculty also agree that something needs to be done to intervene with bullying? Are there faculty members who

think students should work this out for themselves, that bullying is not an education problem, that it makes kids tougher, and so on?

4. If bullying is to be addressed at your school, what is the first step that needs to be taken to make sure the entire faculty is on board? Is it possible to get the entire faculty on board at your school? If not, where do you start?

CHAPTER 3: WHAT STUDENTS MUST KNOW

1. Do the students at your school feel safe? If not, is bullying a part of the problem? How many students would have to feel that the school is not safe for faculty to consider school safety an issue?

2. Do the students feel the faculty cares if bullying goes on? What evidence is there to support this?

3. If a student was bullied at your school, would that student tell faculty or staff? What makes you think this? If a student would tell, which faculty members would that student feel comfortable enough to tell? Which faculty would the student not tell, and why?

4. Is there a structure in place that encourages the reporting of bullying? If there is, is it effective? How would you know? Do students, other than a student who has been the victim of bullying, ever report that bullying has occurred? Are bystanders encouraged to report bullying?

CHAPTER 4: BULLIES AND VICTIMS

1. If bullying occurs at your school, is it considered to be only a problem between the bully and the victim? Other than prevention campaigns, has anything ever been done in a bullying

incident that includes more than merely the bully and the victim . . . that includes the social context?

2. If bullying occurs in a social context, then who, besides the obvious victim, is affected by bullying? What impact does bullying have on the culture at your school?

3. What potential impact could bystanders have on the culture of your school if they were included in the solution? Do bystanders have the right to be included?

CHAPTER 5: BRAIN RESEARCH

1. If different parts of the brain perform different tasks, and if you see that there are certain types of tasks that a student has trouble with, then should you take the time to find ways to address those specific problem areas? Can you be successful with a student otherwise?

2. What implications can you see in the fact that the brain will monitor novel processes in the right hemisphere and shift the monitoring of routine processes to the left hemisphere? What implications could this have for the classroom?

3. If novelty is processed in the right hemisphere and routine is processed in the left hemisphere, as we go from novel tasks to routine tasks isn't the locus of control shifting from one part of the brain to another? If the brain functions in that manner, can we influence this shift at will? Can we shift the locus of control intentionally? How could that potentially help us in both teaching and monitoring student behavior?

CHAPTER 6: EMOTIONAL INTELLIGENCE

1. In this chapter it is asserted that emotional intelligence is learned and that it has typically been learned through

modeling. It is also asserted that emotional intelligence is being modeled in fewer homes, even homes where parents do have a high level of emotional intelligence themselves. Do you agree or disagree with those assertions, and what evidence do you see that causes you to agree or to disagree?

2. What are some of the strategies that could be systematically utilized in your school or in your community for modeling emotional intelligence? What already exists? What possibilities could exist?

3. If, as this chapter indicates, emotional intelligence can be taught, what aspects need to be taught to bullies and potential bullies? Likewise, what aspects need to be taught to victims and potential victims?

CHAPTER 7: EMOTIONAL INTELLIGENCE AND DECISION MAKING

1. This chapter asserts that emotions are a driving force in the decisions we make. What decisions have you made this week? Reflect on how your emotions might have been involved in these decisions.

2. What discipline problems have you seen in your classroom or in your school this week? How are emotions tied into the decisions these students made that landed them in trouble?

3. This chapter asserts that motivation is completely dependent on emotions, that it is what we love and what excites us that motivates us to action of any kind. Do you agree with that assertion? What evidence do you see that causes you to agree or disagree?

4. What are the ways you utilize emotions in your classroom to motivate students? What are some other ways you can think of to utilize emotions to motivate students?

CHAPTER 8: IMPACT BIAS

1. In this chapter it is asserted that impact bias is what causes us to think that the events in our lives will have more of an impact than they typically do have. Have you noted this in the students, especially the teenagers, that you see? What are some of the instances where you have noted this?

2. This chapter points out that our psychological immune systems help us cope with the decisions we make, and it is easier to cope with the finality of a situation or a decision than with the ongoing uncertainty of making a decision that is not final . . . that we can change. Have you noted this in events in your life? Have you noted this in events with students?

3. This chapter asserts that the psychological immune system can be impacted more by a group than it can by an individual. What evidence can you see that this is true with students? How can this be utilized in dealing with students and student attitudes?

CHAPTER 9: THE LIMBIC SYSTEM

1. This chapter discusses the fact that emotions are controlled in the limbic system, that routine processes of the brain are controlled in the left hemisphere, and that by utilizing routine we can actually shift the locus of control out of the limbic system. Numerous examples were given about how we do this. Can you think of and discuss some examples of how this can be beneficial with students at your school?

2. This chapter discusses several instances relating to how language has been used to shift the locus of control out of the limbic system to move someone out of panic or out of trauma. Can you think of examples of how stories or language are utilized now in your school or your classroom to do this? Can you think of additional possibilities for this?

3. In this chapter we discussed four conditions that create stress: novelty, unpredictability, low sense of control, and threat to ego. We also discussed some situations that create stress. Can you think of some students in your classroom or in your school who are under high levels of stress? Can you think of ways that you can address novelty, unpredictability, low sense of control, or threat to ego to reduce the stress level for these students?   ·

4. In this chapter the sense of smell was briefly discussed. Can you think of ways odor has an impact on how students treat each other? Can you devise any plans to address that issue?

CHAPTER 10: THE CONNECTIONS THAT BIND US

1. Can you think back to the significant connections you had in your life growing up? What influences did those connections have on your life?

2. Are there currently students in your classroom or in your school that seem to have no significant positive connections in their lives? What are the issues that have caused this?

3. Think about all the roles that your students play in their lives already. What roles do they have that are conducive to forming positive connections? What can be done to further that possibility for your students?

CHAPTER 11: BUILDING CONNECTIONS

1. This chapter discusses some possible strategies for building connections between students and significant adults. What structures already exist to do this in your school? What other potential strategies could exist with minimal effort? What strategies could exist with some planning and coordination?

2. Also discussed in this chapter are strategies to build connections between and among students. Again, what strategies already exist? What strategies could exist with minimal effort? What strategies could exist with some planning and coordination?

3. There are also other connections that many people have in their lives. These include connections with a religious belief, a group, a cause, a sports team, a neighborhood, or a special interest of some kind. What strategies exist for learning what connections students already have? What strategies exist for utilizing existing connections to support students or to build other connections?

4. Of all the strategies you have discussed, which could effectively be utilized in your classroom? Which could be utilized at your grade level or in your wing or hallway at your school? Which strategies could be implemented schoolwide?

5. How would you determine if the strategies you implement at any level are being effective? What criteria would you use to support this?

CHAPTER 12: BUILDING EMOTIONAL INTELLIGENCE

1. One key step in building emotional intelligence is to build a better emotional vocabulary. Such a vocabulary not only allows students to express what they are feeling and understand what others are feeling but also truly gives the students insight into what they are feeling. It allows a student to broaden her horizons as to possible emotions. If students don't have the word for it, they generally don't have the concept. When a student moves into your classroom, how do you know what level of emotional vocabulary that student already possesses?

2. Do you have strategies in your classroom to determine emotional vocabulary? If so, what are they? What could be done so that you do have an idea?

3. What strategies already exist to help students create a broader emotional vocabulary? What strategies exist to give students an understanding of these concepts? What strategies could be devised that would fit into already existing curriculum or already existing activities?

4. Another key in emotional intelligence is to understand how emotions impact our lives. Do students understand the role of emotions in both the big decisions and the everyday decisions they make? Do they understand the role of emotions in motivation? What criteria would you use to determine this?

5. How could you get this point across in your classroom? What existing activities or lessons could these ideas easily fit with?

6. In what ways do you utilize emotions to generate student motivation? What strategies could you incorporate to systematically achieve this? How do emotions influence your own motivation?

CHAPTER 13: EMOTIONAL TRIGGERS

1. There are certain situations and certain habits of thinking that set off emotional triggers in all of us. Some of these are minor, but sometimes they are problematic. Think about what sets you off, or what sets off someone you care about. Are there certain triggers you can identify?

2. Can you identify students in your classroom who have emotional triggers that lead to destructive or disruptive behaviors? How are you aware of these? Are there students who have behaviors that are problematic in the classroom and you do not know whether there are emotional triggers that set these off? How can you determine this? What steps would you take?

3. How would you know if emotional triggers that are created by destructive or unproductive thought habits set off certain behaviors in students? Are there ways you could learn this? What steps or strategies would need to be taken?

4. What strategies could be devised to manage the emotional triggers you find so they do not get to the point of being destructive or disruptive? How can you intervene? What strategies could be devised to avoid these situations? What strategies could be devised to remove students from these situations? What strategies could be devised to help the students cope with these situations?

5. If and when you identify emotional triggers that set students off, are the students also aware of these triggers? How can you make them aware? What strategies can you give the students to know when this is happening or about to happen? What strategies can you give the students to avoid these situations, to get themselves out of these situations, and to manage these situations?

CHAPTER 14: CREATING AN OUTWARD FOCUS

1. Helping students look outside themselves helps students learn empathy for others, helps them build connections with others, and helps them learn what is important in their own lives. How do you know if a student is focused only on himself or has some focus outside himself as well? What criteria would you use to judge that?

2. What opportunities already exist in your classroom or in your school that can support building an outward focus in students? What opportunities could exist with a little planning? Helping someone younger than yourself is a ready-made scenario for creating an outward focus. Is it possible to develop such strategies with teachers of younger children in your building?

3. What opportunities in your community exist to help build such an outward focus for students? Are parents aware of these? How can we generate or promote family and community efforts to build or promote such opportunities?

4. What strategies can be incorporated to help students think about and understand the importance of reaching out and helping others? Into what existing activities and lessons could such an outward focus be incorporated?

CHAPTER 15: THE MAGIC OF ROUTINE

1. Routine is such a critical strategy to use for students because it can literally shift the locus of control out of the part of the brain that is distraught or anxious. Routine settles and calms, allowing the student to function. Some students need more help with structure and routine than others. Can you think of students in your class or your school that could benefit from more structure and routine? What structure and routine can be put into a daily structure for those students?

2. Having routine ways of responding to a crisis or to a novel situation is also important. Can you identify students in your class or your school who do not have good problem-solving skills, who do not have routines that help them manage crisis or novel situations? How can you recognize these students? What steps can you take in your classroom to support students' learning such routines so they have more control and self-regulation over their problems and their lives?

3. Can you recognize students in your classroom who have routine thought patterns or thought habits that are destructive or disruptive? Are there strategies you can incorporate in your classroom to challenge and change these to more productive thought habits? Can parents be utilized to address these negative thought habits? Are there other resources, such as a school counselor or school social worker, who could help with these issues?

4. Stress is a serious issue that both interferes with student productivity and creates classroom problems. How can establishing routines (including daily routines, response routines,

and thought routines) be utilized to reduce or manage student stress?

CHAPTER 16: FINAL THOUGHTS

1. Bullying exists in all societies. It often exists because of differences in people . . . differences in students. What strategies already exist in your school, in your classroom that promote diversity or encourage acceptance of differences? What strategies could be devised to help students learn that it is difference and novelty that make people interesting, that make life exciting?

2. Our society changes at a rapid rate. Technology sees to that. Change involves letting go of past ideas and past comforts, living with a period of anxiety, and embracing the eventual growth that comes. The brain changes at a rapid rate. Every experience we have changes the brain. As we practice new experiences, the brain forms new neural pathways. How can we best utilize this information in our schools, in our classrooms, with our students to help them deal with change effectively and to promote the kinds of changes that make schools safe and productive environments for all students? What step-by-step strategies do we need to develop to achieve this? The following worksheets are designed to facilitate the promotion and planning of such strategies.

Where Do We Go From Here?
External Interventions
What Role Can Parents Play?

If bullying is a problem in our school, and if we really intend to address this issue, then parents must be an integral part of the solution. How can we achieve that?

What strategies do we need to utilize to gain parent support and involvement?	What specific steps need to be taken to implement this strategy?	Who will be responsible for initiating and/or sustaining these steps?	What is a realistic time line for this step or this phase of the step?	How will we assess the effectiveness of our initiative? How will we know that we accomplished our goal?
1.				
2.				
3.				

Where Do We Go From Here?
External Interventions
What Role Does the Faculty Play?

If bullying is a problem in our school, and if we really intend to address this issue, then faculty and staff must be willing to take some specific actions. How can we achieve that?

What strategies do we need to utilize as faculty and staff to achieve this goal?	What specific steps need to be taken to implement this strategy?	Who will be responsible for initiating and/or sustaining these steps?	What is a realistic time line for this step or this phase of the step?	How will we assess the effectiveness of our initiative? How will we know that we accomplished our goal?
1.				
2.				
3.				

Where Do We Go From Here?
External Interventions
What Role Do Students Play?

If bullying is a problem in our school, and if we really intend to address this issue, then we must get students involved as a part of the solution. How can we achieve that?

What strategies do we need to utilize to get students involved in achieving this goal?	What specific steps need to be taken to implement this strategy?	Who will be responsible for initiating and/or sustaining these steps?	What is a realistic time line for this step or this phase of the step?	How will we assess the effectiveness of our initiative? How will we know that we accomplished our goal?
1.				
2.				
3.				

Where Do We Go From Here?
External Interventions
How Can We Build Connections for Students?

If bullying is a problem in our school, and if we really intend to address this issue, then helping students build connections in their lives is an important part of the solution. How can we achieve that?

What strategies do we need to utilize to help students build significant connections?	What specific steps need to be taken to implement this strategy?	Who will be responsible for initiating and/or sustaining these steps?	What is a realistic time line for this step or this phase of the step?	How will we assess the effectiveness of our initiative? How will we know that we accomplished our goal?
1.				
2.				
3.				

Where Do We Go From Here?
External Interventions
How Can We Help Students Build Emotional Intelligence?

If bullying is a problem in our school, and if we really intend to address this issue, then helping students develop emotional intelligence is an important part of the solution. How can we achieve that?

What strategies do we need to utilize to help students develop emotional intelligence?	What specific steps need to be taken to implement this strategy?	Who will be responsible for initiating and/or sustaining these steps?	What is a realistic time line for this step or this phase of the step?	How will we assess the effectiveness of our initiative? How will we know that we accomplished our goal?
1.				
2.				
3.				

Where Do We Go From Here?
External Interventions
How Can We Help Students Recognize and Manage Emotional Triggers?

If bullying is a problem in our school, and if we really intend to address this issue, then helping students to both recognize and manage their emotional triggers is an important part of the solution. How can we achieve that?

What strategies do we need to utilize to help students recognize and manage their emotional triggers?	What specific steps need to be taken to implement this strategy?	Who will be responsible for initiating and/or sustaining these steps?	What is a realistic time line for this step or this phase of the step?	How will we assess the effectiveness of our initiative? How will we know that we accomplished our goal?
1.				
2.				
3.				

Where Do We Go From Here?
External Interventions
How Can We Help Students Focus Outside Themselves?

If bullying is a problem in our school, and if we really intend to address this issue, then helping students to focus outside rather than inside is an important part of the solution. How can we achieve that?

What strategies do we need to utilize to help students focus outside themselves?	What specific steps need to be taken to implement this strategy?	Who will be responsible for initiating and/or sustaining these steps?	What is a realistic time line for this step or this phase of the step?	How will we assess the effectiveness of our initiative? How will we know that we accomplished our goal?
1.				
2.				
3.				

Where Do We Go From Here?
External Interventions
How Can We Help Students Build and Utilize Routine and Structure?

If bullying is a problem in our school, and if we really intend to address this issue, then helping students to recognize the importance of routine and to utilize it is an important part of the solution. How can we achieve that?

What strategies do we need to utilize to help students recognize and utilize routine and structure?	What specific steps need to be taken to implement this strategy?	Who will be responsible for initiating and/or sustaining these steps?	What is a realistic time line for this step or this phase of the step?	How will we assess the effectiveness cf our initiative? How will we know that we accomplished our goal?
1.				
2.				
3.				

Where Do We Go From Here?

How Can We _____ _____ ?

Interventions

(Additional Worksheet)

If bullying is a problem in our school, and if we really intend to address this issue, then how can we achieve that?

What additional strategies do we need to utilize?	What specific steps need to be taken to implement this strategy?	Who will be responsible for initiating and/or sustaining these steps?	What is a realistic time line for this step or this phase of the step?	How will we assess the effectiveness of our initiative? How will we know that we accomplished our goal?
1.				
2.				
3.				

REFERENCES

Amen, D. G. (1999). *Change your brain, change your life: The break-through program for conquering anxiety, depression, obsessiveness, anger, and impulsiveness.* New York: Three Rivers Press.

Cottle, T. J. (2004, April). *Defying your brain: On rethinking the nature of normal behavior.* Learning and the Brain Conference. Boston: Public Information Resources.

Fowler-Finn, T. (2001). Student stability vs. mobility. *School Administrator, 58,(7),* 36–40.

Frankl, V. (1963). *Man's search for meaning.* Boston: Beacon Press.

Gilbert, D. T. (2002, November). *Why the secret of happiness is a secret to adults and children.* Learning and the Brain Conference. Boston: Public Information Resources.

Goldberg, E. (2001). *The executive brain: Frontal lobes and the civilized mind.* New York: Oxford University Press.

Goleman, D. (1995). *Emotional intelligence: Why it can matter more than IQ.* New York: Bantam Books.

Hallowell, E. M. (2002). *The childhood roots of adult happiness: Five steps to help kids create and sustain lifelong joy.* New York: Ballantine Books.

Harris, S., & Petrie, G. F. (2003). *Bullying: The bullies, the victims, the bystanders.* Lanham, MA: Scarecrow Press.

Hawkins, J. D. (1993). *It's everybody's business.* Pamona, CA: California State Polytechnic University Southwest Regional Laboratory Developmental Research & Programs TARGET.

Juvonen, J. (2004, March 1). Everyone loves a bully. *Psychology Today,* 20.

Lovre, C. (2004, February). Workshop on Crisis Intervention, Trauma, and Stress. Crisis Management Institute. Bloomington, IN: National Education Service.

Lupien, S. J. (2004, April). *The impact of socioeconomic status on children's stress hormone levels, emotional processing, and memory performance.* Learning and the Brain Conference. Boston: Public Information Resources.

Nelson, P. S., Simoni, J. M., & Adelman, H. S. (1996). Mobility and school functioning in the early grades. *Journal of Educational Research, 89,* 365–369.

Olweus, D. (1993). *Bullying at school: What we know and what we can do.* Oxford, UK: Blackwell Publishing.

School Board News. (2002, May 7). *Chicago schools use many strategies to reduce student mobility.* Alexandria, VA: National School Boards Association.

Silver, H. F. (2000). *So each may learn: Integrating learning styles and multiple intelligence.* Alexandria, VA: Association for Supervision and Curriculum Development.

Stover, D. (2000). The mobility mess of students who move. *Education Digest, 66*(3), 61–64.

Varlas, L. (2002). *Slowing the revolving door: Schools reach out to mobile families.* Alexandria, VA: Association for Supervision and Curriculum Development.

Wedekind, C., Seebeck, T., Bettens, F., & Paepke, A. J. (1995). MHC-dependent mate preferences in humans. *Proceedings of the Royal Society of London, 260,* 245–249.

ABOUT THE AUTHOR

Gary R. Plaford is director of social services at the Monroe County Community School Corporation. He has presented at numerous state conferences on the topic of bullying and has taught classes at Indiana University on bullying, child and adolescent issues, and understanding behavior.